TRAVELS WITH WILLIE
ADVENTURE CYCLIST

Also by Willie Weir

Spokesongs: Bicycle Adventures on Three Continents

TRAVELS
WITH
WILLIE
ADVENTURE CYCLIST

WILLIE WEIR

pineleaf productions
Seattle, Washington

Travels with Willie: Adventure Cyclist

Printed in the United States of America

10 9 8 7 6 5 4 3 2 1

ISBN 10: 0-9656792-8-4
ISBN 13: 978-0-9656792-8-2

Most of the material in this work has been previously published in *Adventure
Cyclist* magazine, a publication of the Adventure Cycling Association.

Book design by Kat Marriner
All photographs by Willie Weir unless noted

Published by Pineleaf Productions
Seattle, Washington

Visit www.WillieWeir.com

TO THE MEMBERS of
the Adventure Cycling Association

VULPES VULPES

30 L

BANKA E SHTETIT SHQIPTAR

10

DH

10

भारत INDIA
1.00
1992

Dogu
Sariot
10 km
Carsanba
7 km
Kardoy
Domanis

Tunsba

Gumey

Tuncbilok
Tavianli Ernakuidede
Gamamba
Haymeana
manastir
kandol
Sey
Songui 17k

durmi
8k
nookauk

Kuzey

1996

25.00
НАРОДНА НА ОДЕКФ ОТ СРЪБСКО-БЪЛГАРСКАТА ВОЙНА
БЪЛГАРИЯ · BULGARIA

2 भारत

3

My name is Themba
Igama lami ngingu Themba
BHEKI MAZIBUKO & THEMBA NGCWAZA
KwaZulu Monument
Council
P. O. Box 523
ULundi
3838

79-1898
ESIKHWE
? ALT+GA
41558
35
LEN
VAN SCHALKWYCE'S
× ARCHEOLOGICAL PEAR+
SITE + CAMP
MIDDLE
DRIFT
BHEKI / THEMBA NGC
TUGELA MAZIBU
KRANSKOP
STANGER
BLV
TONGAAT
VERULUM
MT CAVELOMBE

3

I PAGUHEN PRURËSIT ME TË PARË

3

CONTENTS

PROLOGUE

BEYOND BROOKGLEN WAY

STARING INTENTLY DOWN the ever-so-slightly sloped drive-way I gripped the handlebars of my Schwinn Stingray with all my might. I turned my head to the right. Training wheels were absent. I checked left. Parental stabilizing unit was attached. No traffic anywhere to be seen. No sign of the neighbor's large German Shepherd.

With a nod of my head I indicated, "OK Dad. Hit it. We're ready to roll."

My bike wobbled down the driveway and picked up speed to just under five miles an hour and a thousand thoughts ran through my brain:

"Got to make a left hand turn at the end of the driveway. Still no traffic. Maybe I should signal. *No!* Keep both hands on the bars. What if I fall? They just recently paved the road and I'll be picking gravel out of my knees for months. Safely on the street now. Gaining speed. Woa! A little wobbly there. This is great Dad … Dad? … Dad!!!! Mayday. Mayday. Parental stabilizing unit is detached. We're going down. We are going *down*. No. Wait. Stabilizing. I've got control. Picking up more speed. I can do this. I *am* doing this. I am riding down *my* street all by *myself* … I am *King of the world!*"

OK. Maybe it wasn't as cinematic as that. But if you are at all like me, you remember the exact second when you learned how to ride a bike. It was a rite of passage. It was a childhood declaration of independence.

There were limits however. I was allowed to ride up and down the street and in and around the cul-de-sac, but under no circumstances was I to go beyond Brookglen Way. That was the edge of my cycling universe as established by Mom.

So the first chance I got. What did I do? You guessed it. I zoomed past that sign at twelve and a half miles an hour and into a lifetime of adventure. That Schwinn Stingray wasn't a bicycle. It was a magic carpet.

I've been cycling beyond Brookglen Way ever since, progressing from local to national to global journeys. The bicycles I've pedaled have changed over the years. I outgrew a few. One was stolen. One just plain wore out. The one I ride now is custom built.

But they've all been magic.

CROSSING THE STREET

EVERYTHING FELT FOREIGN, from the humidity in the air, to the orchids blooming, to the hustle and bustle of scooters, taxis, and *tuk-tuks* (small three-wheeled taxis). Everything except what was on my plate—two eggs (over easy) and white toast with strawberry jam. There was nothing on that plate that said "Thailand". Yet it was the only breakfast item available. I perused the other tables. Four couples. My guess? Australians, Germans, Dutch and Canadians. All eating the same breakfast, all reading the same guidebook.

Why?

It surely wasn't the case of not having an alternative.

There had to be a thousand different places to eat within walking distance of this backpacker's lodge.

In a word—familiarity. The need to grasp hold of something from home while surrounded by foreignness, and believe me—two eggs, toast and jam are familiar and comforting.

Out there, beyond the English menu, strawberry jam, and traveler's message boards, was the pulsating metropolis of Bangkok, the capitol of a country that speaks a tonal language written in a script that appears to be artistic doodling. Where elephants roam and forty-seven of the 168 species of snake are venomous, where Buddhas sit in temples and boxers are allowed to use their feet. And speaking of feet, don't point them at anyone, that would be offensive. And don't clear your plate as your mother taught you, that would be offensive, too.

They don't call it culture shock for nothing. Ever made the mistake of diving into the crystal clear water of a mountain lake or stream on a hot summer day before testing the temperature of the water? I did. In Glacier National Park, in August. One moment I was in a John Denver Rocky Mountain High-like bliss, stripping off my clothes and the next I was drowning, two feet from shore, my arms barely able to move; my mouth opened in a silent scream of frigid horror.

The beginning of a journey can feel the same way. You are so damn excited when you leave for the airport. Then you miss your connection. You temporarily misplace your passport, and you're convinced you've left the stove on at home. You finally get off the airplane after no sleep, three bad meals and six in-flight movies, and a wall of humidity hits you. You are overwhelmed with strange sights and sounds, none of which you understand. You retrieve your bike and baggage and somehow manage to load it onto a bus or taxi or *tuk-tuk* and race screaming into a giant traffic jam of steel and humanity. It's exciting and exhilarating and terrifying all at the same time.

You finally make your way to a backpacker's lodge or hotel, highly recommended by friends or your favorite guidebook series, check in, throw your baggage into the corner and collapse onto the bed.

Once you wake up, you have every intention to explore hidden streets and alleys. Find out where the locals eat and sit elbow-to-elbow with them, laughing and slurping up the soup of the day. No organized bus tours or walks. You're going native.

That's your best intention anyway.

And yet there you sit, observing the spectacle from the safety of your table at the backpacker's lodge, with your two eggs, toast and strawberry jam.

The problem is there are so many backpacker lodges throughout Thailand that it is possible to travel from one end of the country to the other without ever having to leave that safety net of familiarity. You can see the entire country in the company of other travelers just like you.

Not that I'm referring to myself in the above scenario. Not me. I'm a columnist for *Adventure Cyclist* magazine. I'm intrepid. I'm unique.

I'm lying.

I'm no different than most travelers. As much as I hate to admit it, I like the familiar. Given the choice between staying in a hut or a tent, surrounded by people I can't understand and sleeping in a clean bed in lodging where English is spoken, I'll usually take the more comfortable of the two. I'll hate myself later for having done so, but I'll do it.

As many times as I've traveled, the beginning of a trip is always awkward for me. It reminds me of the first day of school—excitement mixed with dread. But most of all, the burning desire to fit in. To be wearing the right clothes and carrying the right lunch box ... or is it brown bags this year? Just let me get through the day without looking stupid.

That's why I choose to travel by bicycle. It forces me to be the traveler that I long to be, one that moves beyond the familiar to the uncomfortable.

The bicycle leads me into places and situations where familiarity is not an option: to roadside restaurants that haven't seen a foreigner in years, to local festivals not listed and recommended in the *Lonely Planet*, to the shade of a tree shared with local school kids, to a police station or a monastery and a safe place to sleep.

I know this. I've lived this—time and time again since the age of nineteen.

Yet it is a lesson that must be relearned every journey.

I woke up the next morning and wandered down to the dining area of the backpacker's lodge. I saw the same couples eating the same breakfast while consulting the same guidebooks.

This scared me into action.

I managed to break free from the safe confines of the backpacker's lodge and made my way across the street to a tiny roll top restaurant with little card tables and plastic chairs.

The beautiful woman in an apron and cap interpreted my gestures and began to work.

Palm oil hit the hot wok, quickly followed by garlic and hot peppers. She used a wide and deep metal spatula as if it were a whole drawer full of utensils. A tear-inducing cloud of steam rose, diffused in the yellow glow of early morning light. Fish sauce and rice followed, and Thai basil and three or four other items I couldn't begin to recognize.

I began to notice the symphony of sounds around me: the scrapping sound of the spatula, the loud slurping of the man next to me hugging his bowl of noodles, the laughter of groups of uniformed kids walking to school, the high nasal honks of *tuk-tuks* delivering produce or shoppers or both, all amidst the dull roar of a billions other sounds of the city.

With a flourish, the young cook served up my breakfast on a plastic plate along with a cup of hot tea.

I took one bite.

I had been in Thailand for twenty-four hours and had finally arrived. The journey could begin.

You can travel half way around the world, across oceans and continents. But to reap travel's true rewards—you still have to cross the street.

PASSPORT TO ADVENTURE

Would you leave on a long journey without taking your passport? Neither would I. But I'm not talking about that wallet-sized document. I'm speaking of the two-wheeled, human-powered vehicle that has propelled me into adventure all across the globe.

I am not an avid cyclist. I am an avid traveler who has discovered that cycling is the best way to see the world. Bicycles have a way of turning trips into adventures. I can't remember ever meeting someone who has traveled by bicycle who didn't agree.

I call the bicycle "one of the last innocent forms of transportation". The bicycle has managed to roll through history with its wholesome image unscathed.

To the skeptics, I relate this story:

On a late July evening in a small town in the province of New Brunswick, I approached a modest looking home and knocked on the door. I was over 5,000 miles into my bicycle journey across Canada. There was no local campground and the sun was minutes away from setting.

A girl in her early teens answered the door.

"Hi. My name's Willie," I said. "I'm cycling across Canada and I was wondering if I could set my tent up somewhere on your lawn."

She told me that I would have to ask her mother and disappeared back into the house.

When her mother came to the door I decided not to go to the trouble of a long explanation and simply said.

"I was wondering if it would be possible if I could pitch my tent on your property for the night."

The woman's brow furrowed as if I was a 300-pound linebacker standing on her doorstep trying to sell Girl Scout cookies. I knew immediately that permission would be denied.

"Why our yard?" she asked. "Haven't you tried to find a campground? I think there's one in the next town about twenty-five kilometers away."

"I'm sorry. I didn't mean to impose. I'll try somewhere else." I turned to walk away.

"Wait," she said. "Where are you from? You have an accent."

"I'm from Seattle, Washington."

At that moment the woman looked passed my shoulder and saw my bicycle in the fading light.

"On *that?*"

"Yes", I said. "I started my journey in May and … "

She cut me off mid-sentence.

"Oh my God!" she sputtered. "Of course you can camp on our lawn. There is a nice flat spot behind our garage."

I thanked her and wheeled my bicycle over to the freshly mowed lawn. Because I had just cycled across Northern Ontario during peak black fly season, I could set up my tent in about forty-eight seconds. As I was tossing my gear into my nylon dome, the woman came running out of the house.

"I'm so sorry," she said.

She's changed her mind I thought. I'm going to be hittin' the road in the dark.

"I can't believe I didn't think of this. Come over here." She beckoned me to the garage.

She opened the side door.

"As you can see, we don't park our car here. My husband uses this as a workspace. Well, he used to work in here. Now he just plays golf and sits and watches … oh, that's too much information. Anyway. The floor is carpeted and it may rain this evening. It is silly for you to sleep in a tent when this is available."

I wasn't going to argue. The tent came down and I now had my sleeping bag laid out on thick shag carpeting. I leaned back in comfort against a tool cabinet, my back cushioned with a down pillow brought from the house. Compared to my cramped tent, this was "The Ritz".

I took out a book to read, and hadn't even finished a page when there came a knock at the door.

"I'm so sorry." The woman peeked her head in the door. "I can't believe I didn't think of this."

I followed her back outside.

"Do you see the trailer parked out back? Well, my son sleeps out there, but he's gone for a couple of weeks. It's silly for you to sleep in our garage when there is a comfortable bed for you."

Actually, I'd grown quite fond of my garage suite. But I didn't want to argue with hospitality. I began stuffing my sleeping bag back into its stuff sack.

Fifteen minutes later I lounged on a double bed with a down comforter and clicked on the lamp by my bedside table to continue reading.

There was a timid knock at the door.

What possibly could be next?

The woman smiled as I opened the door.

"I'm so sorry. I know you have food with you. But I just cooked up a big steak dinner and we would be honored if you would come and share a meal with us."

I would like to say that it was my charming personality that led me to dine with this delightful family in New Brunswick. But my charming personality had struck out. It was my bicycle that made the difference. In those two seconds she had gone from seeing a vagrant on her front porch to seeing an adventurer.

On the same journey across Canada I cycled into the city limits of Montreal, Quebec. In less than two hours a dozen people stopped me to ask if I had a place to stay, offering their homes or apartments. I couldn't believe how friendly these people were.

Montreal happened to be the one city where I already had a place to stay. Gaton was a friend of a high school buddy of mine and he welcomed me with open arms to his apartment.

When I told him about all the invitations he replied, "It is *Saint-Jean-Baptiste Day*. Everybody is in a good mood and ready to party."

Gaton had a previous engagement, so he left me with a key and told me he would meet me later.

I decided to take a walk through the old downtown neighborhoods. It was a beautiful summer evening and many streets had been blocked off to traffic. Tables of food and drink spilled out into the streets as whole neighborhoods celebrated.

I appreciated the freedom of wandering a city without having to worry about my bicycle and my gear (all safe back at Gaton's apartment).

But my reception was less than congenial. Adults and children ignored me as I walked through these neighborhood celebrations. Every non-verbal message stated that these were private functions and meant to remain that way.

What had happened to the overly friendly people of Montreal? Was I simply walking through the wrong neighborhood?

Then it dawned on me. I had forgotten my passport.

Fifteen minutes later I walked back through the same neighborhood, wheeling my gear-laden bicycle.

People smiled, some waived. A slender man in his forties sporting a beret approached me and invited me to sit down and have something to eat. He poured me a glass of wine.

I finally mustered up the courage to ask him if he had seen me earlier.

"Yes I did. But I thought you were a tourist. Now I see that you are a traveler. You have earned the right to sit at this table."

We lifted our glasses and toasted the day.

That journey was many years ago. Since then my bicycle has opened doors to strange and exotic worlds. To homes, huts and hovels across the world. To fiestas in Mexico, festivals in India, and ceremonies in tribal South Africa.

People often ask me if I would consider traveling without my bicycle.

I simply reply:

"And leave my passport at home? You've got to be kidding."

AT A LOSS FOR WORDS

BIKES AND BOOKS are a fabulous combo. They both allow one to explore, to wander, to visit exotic places, and to discover new worlds and passions. Both require effort to propel the participant forward. Both can be artfully made or mass-produced.

I do my share of reading at home, but it is mostly newspaper and magazine articles. Books just read better when you're on a journey. Your body is tired from a day of pedaling and your mind is free from the workaday stress. Give me a tent, a headlamp, and a good book and I am one happy camper.

The journey also brings its own perspective to the pages your soaking up. I read Peter Jenkins's *A Walk Across America* while I was cycling across America. I read *Midnight's Children* by Salman Rushdie while pedaling around India, experiencing the same heat and smelling the exotic fragrances he described. I finished Nelson Mandela's biography while pedaling through the former homeland of the Ciskei where Mandella was born, hearing his native tongue, Xhosa, spoken as I closed the book. In New Zealand I was reading the classic, *Mutiny on the Bounty*. There was a mention of Fletcher Christian gazing up at the Magellanic Clouds, a couple of galaxies one can see with the naked eye in the southern hemisphere. I turned off my headlamp and there they were, two fuzzy splotches in the night sky. It gave me literary shivers.

The problem with books from a cyclist's perspective is their weight. Unless you are out of your mind or have quads of steel, you don't throw into your panniers the dozen books you've been dying to read. There's usually some sort of guidebook you'd like to pack, which then leaves room for one or two pleasure books tops. This is unfortunate. But if you are traveling in a country whose language is predominantly English, you can often pull into a used bookstore, sell the book you've just finished, and emerge with a new gem.

In other parts of the world, finding reading material, once you've exhausted your limited supply, can be a challenge—if not downright maddening.

When Kat and I cycled in Cuba for three months, we each brought a book with us. We quickly ingested them and traded. After a couple of weeks we traded again and re-read our first choices. We searched and inquired at every stop, but there was no English reading material to be found on the island. We read our guidebook, over and over and over. You know you are getting desperate when you find yourself reading the warning label on your camp stove fuel bottle ... for the fifth time.

We ended up pedaling out of our way to a resort on the coast in hopes of finding English-speaking guests and their coveted works of fiction. We arrived during the Sunday brunch hour and found ourselves seated next to a group of Canadians. We did the obligatory chitchat and then cut to the chase: "Would you happen to have any reading material that you could part with?"

"Oh, I bet we could dig up something," replied a woman from Manitoba with an enormous sun hat.

We were so excited we could barely stay seated. We wanted to dash into her room and ransack it, leaving no printed word behind.

After about twenty minutes she returned to our table with a plastic bag. We were giddy.

Inside were three copies of Canadian *Readers Digest* (just as schlocky as *Reader's Digest*, but with a Canadian flag on the cover) and two paperbacks that could only be described as romance/horse novels.

We didn't reveal our disappointment and truth be told, we read every single word contained in that plastic bag—twice!

On our most recent trip in Turkey, English books were available, but at a price that left us speechless and later bookless. Used paperbacks were going for twenty-five U.S. dollars each, forcing us to choose between eating and reading. On a bicycle trip, feeding one's soul takes a back seat to filling one's belly. The paperbacks remained on the shelf and we resorted to reading our guidebook ... over and over and over.

"Hey honey, has that label worn off the fuel bottle?"

I know there are people who will read this and ask, "Why don't you get a laptop and load it with e-books?" I'll admit that I'm a Luddite. Even when I finally break down and join the laptop-packing adventurers, I'll still want to hold and caress a book with pages. It just feels good.

Before I left on an extended pedal around Central America I went shopping for a good book. After two hours of wandering in a used-book store, I emerged with an old, tattered paperback copy of *Atlas Shrugged* by Ayn Rand. It was one of those books I had always meant to read, but had never gotten around to.

There was one problem. At 1,100 pages, the book just wouldn't fit in my front handlebar bag, which was already stuffed with a camera and extra lenses. After much debate and soul searching, I decided to put my Swiss Army knife to use and slice the book into one hundred-page sections. Desecrating a book in this manner left me queasy, but it was already beginning to fall apart. I was just hastening its inevitable demise.

This allowed me to soak up one hundred pages at a time and then rid myself of the material burden. The more I read, the lighter my load. Why hadn't I thought to employ this method years ago?

The book began slowly, as do many of my bicycle journeys. By the time I'd pedaled through Belize, I'd only managed to get to page 242. But somewhere in Guatemala, the novel sucked me in and I flew through the next 500 pages, tossing each section as I went. Pages 301–399 were used to begin a campfire at 8,000 feet. As I crossed from El Salvador into Nicaragua I had only two more sections of the book. I threw them both into my handlebar bag.

I couldn't wait to get to the end. I went through a set of batteries in my flashlight that night, polishing off pages 900–999. The next morning I tossed the section into a burning pile of rubbish on the side of the road.

My mind wasn't on the scenery or the people around me; it was wrapped up in a novel. It was time to release myself from this work of fiction and get back to the reality of my bicycle journey. After about twenty miles of pedaling, I bought a quart of milk, a bag of cookies and found the shade of a palm tree.

I got comfortable, using my sleeping bag as a pillow, and began to read. But something was wrong. Terribly wrong. The first paragraph was all too familiar. I gazed at the upper right hand corner and saw the page number. It was 900!

I had thrown out the wrong section of the book.

Atlas may have shrugged, but on the edge of a dirt road in Nicaragua … Willie screamed.

THE COIN

$3,200.00. THAT'S THREE thousand two hundred dollars. More than eighty percent of American brides receive a diamond engagement ring and that is the average price paid for this symbol of love.

When I asked Kat Marriner to marry me, she received a small disc of metal worth approximately twenty-five cents: A 500 Italian lira coin. Today, thanks to the euro, it is worthless. In fact, this same coin today is used to scam travelers since it looks strikingly similar to the two-euro coin.

In most publications and social circles I would most definitely be dubbed the cheapest of bastards.

I didn't meet Kat on a bicycle trip. I met her at a Christmas party at the Aurora Highland Ice Skating Arena in Seattle.

I was a bicycle traveler with no particular interest in a long term relationship. But I was dazzled on the ice and soon truly smitten. This was a relationship worth staying put for.

There was a glitch though. I had already planned a bicycle journey through the Balkans and had lined up writing commentaries for the local public radio station.

So four months into a new relationship, I was leaving on a five-month journey.

I hadn't even considered asking Kat to join me. She had never toured by bicycle and I was heading into some high-risk territory.

I waved goodbye to "Kissie Girl" as my nephew then called her, boarded the plane and thought, "You idiot. You are going to regret going on this trip."

And I did—from the moment I arrived in Budapest. I was pedaling through this romantic city, completely depressed.

A couple of weeks later I got a surprise phone call in Ljubljana, the capital city of Slovenia. It was Kat. Not only did she miss me, but wished she could be on the bicycle journey as well.

I told her that this wasn't a decision to make on the fly. "Why don't you take the time to really think this through and I'll call you in a couple of weeks and see if you still feel the same way. Maybe we can work something out."

I hung up the phone and immediately regretted the whole conversation.

"Are you insane? A beautiful woman you are crazy about just offered to quit her job and join you on a bicycle journey and you told her to take some time and think about it?!!!"

Willie Weir—international traveler, commentator—and bachelor for life.

A few days later while pedaling along the border of Italy I couldn't help but think, "Yea. She's going to think it over all right, and quickly decide to dump the "bike guy.""

I had to call her back. But long distance calls from Croatia were insanely expensive. So I rode across the border into Italy where the phone rates were much cheaper.

I tried to use my calling card at the first pay phone I could find, but discovered I needed a local coin to initiate the call. I exchanged five bucks and plunked a 500-lira coin into the slot.

Kat didn't answer ... her machine did.

I immediately blathered something like, "I can't believe I told you to think about it! What I meant to say was *yes!* Please come and join me if you are not already dating a wealthy software engineer. That was a joke, sort of. Talk with you soon ... I hope."

The coin dropped into the return slot when I hung up the phone.

Forty-eight hours of internal turmoil later I again crossed the border into Italy and using the same coin I dialed her number.

She answered.

She said yes.

We'd meet back in Budapest in three weeks.

I hung up the phone and the coin rattled around in the return slot.

I was ecstatic and horrified at the same time. Immediately doubt set in.

"What are you doing? She's never been on a bike trip. She's going to quit her job and three days into the trip she is going to quit you."

Three weeks later I met her at the airport. In that time she had quit her job, given up her apartment, put her belongings in storage and with the help of a couple of my friends, retrofitted my old bike for touring.

The first time she rode a bike with loaded panniers was from the airport into Budapest.

In those three weeks, while cycling through Bosnia, I had decided to ask her to marry me.

And I did … on the banks of the Danube with the Budapest's Royal Castle glowing in the background.

When my brain confirmed that she had indeed said, "Yes" I handed her the 500-lira coin.

"I don't have the money for an engagement ring and diamonds aren't my thing anyway. This is the coin I used to call you to ask you to come and join me. It is the same one I used to hear your answer."

Her smile and the tears in her eyes told me that my frugal token was more than acceptable. She put it in the small homemade cloth bag along with her passport for safekeeping.

The next three months were a roller coaster, both on and off the bikes.

This was not your bed and breakfast tour.

This was the back roads of Romania, Bulgaria and Macedonia—voracious mosquitoes and black flies, nights in a small tent in cornfields with thunderstorms, intestinal maladies and saddle sores, mountain passes on dirt and gravel roads.

I know that each of us swore dozens of times that we'd made a mistake. This just wasn't going to work out.

But there were also wondrous sunsets, fields of flowers and honey, local villagers who took us in like family and effortless descents coasting through the beauty of the Carpathian Mountains.

After three months we had been through ten years' worth of relational trials and reconciliation. Our relationship had been tested on a daily basis and only grew stronger.

By the time we crossed over the border into Albania we were travel-tested and secure.

Then, on a lonely stretch of highway in the mountains of Albania, a jolt of harsh reality.

Three men. A knife and clubs. Screams and panic. And fear—soul-wrenching fear.

It was ninety seconds at most. We found ourselves in the middle of the road, hugging each other, bruised and bloody, victims of highway robbery.

They hadn't taken our bikes, but had grabbed valuables—cameras, a tape recorder, our passports.

Kat gasped. "The coin. My coin. It was in the pouch with my passport."

But what did it matter? We were alive.

Some locals who had heard the commotion had hiked up to the road from their village. They helped drag our bikes to the side of the road and gathered some of our things that had been strewn about.

We sat dazed, holding each other, trying to process what had just happened.

An old woman tapped Kat on the shoulder and held out her hand. In it was a cloth pouch. The robbers had ripped it open and grabbed Kat's passport. It was empty—except for a single 500-lira coin glistening in the midday sun.

Ten years later, Kat wears it on a chain around her neck—a worthless coin that represents a valuable life of adventure, love and devotion.

ADDICTION

I'M SURE EVERY addict has their moment of realization, the moment they feel compelled to confess to themselves and to others that their relationship to a certain substance is out of control.

My confession would sound something like this: "Hi. My name is Willie and I just learned that seventeen percent of my budget for cycling across Canada was spent on ice cream. I am an addict."

And like many addicts, I can recall in detail my relationship with the abused substance.

It all started innocently. In fact, I'm sure it was my mother who introduced me to the stuff—just a dollop of vanilla on top of my first birthday cake. Then there were summer days, trying to dig up enough change to buy a "push-up" from the ice cream man (vanilla and orange sherbet swirled in a cardboard cylinder that you pushed-up with the attached stick, like so much weather caulking).

But I can remember the exact moment when "like" turned the corner to "must have."

It was a hot summer August day in Sacramento, California and my Uncle Joe was visiting from New York state. We walked into an ice cream shop together and studied each and every tub in the display case. I finally decided on chocolate almond and chocolate chip. Uncle Joe grinned at me and said, "Get another scoop."

A triple? No one in my family had ever been allowed to order a triple. Before he could rescind his offer, I requested "Chocolate Killer Overload Fudge" and the guy behind the counter balanced it atop the other two scoops.

Uncle Joe had ordered a triple as well. We sat down at those little plastic schoolhouse-like chairs and consumed six billion calories of ice cream without coming up for air. No sooner had the last bits of cone disappeared into our mouths, Uncle Joe leaned over and asked, "Do you want another?" Here was an adult confirming what I already knew as fact—there was no such thing as too much ice cream.

Uncle Joe had introduced me to excess, but cycling was what fueled the fire of addiction.

When my bike sat idle, I could control my cravings for the most part. I could go a week sometimes without one lick. But on the road on a bicycle trip, my desire, my lust, my absolute need for ice cream bordered on manic. There was just something about that cold combination of milk, fat and sugar that made ice cream the breakfast, lunch, dinner and snack of champions. Soft-serve, home-made, premium, bargain-brand. It didn't matter. The bicycle allowed me to consume grotesquely enormous amounts of it without the aftereffects appearing in rolls of fat and flab on my body.

Ice cream sandwiches were the daily and often hourly indulgence throughout my U.S. cross-country adventure. My buddy Thomas and I were on a tight budget, so premium ice cream was off-limits. At twenty-five cents a pop for the cheapest brand, these waxed-paper wrapped treats, dug out from the frosty depths of convenience stores across America adhered to our theme, "Quantity matters!" The gorging peaked on my birthday somewhere in Minnesota, when Thomas bought a package of twenty and we ate them all in one sitting. Since it was my birthday, Thomas got nine, I ate eleven.

On another trip, I went out of my way in Vermont to pedal up to the Mecca of high-fat premium ice cream ... the Ben & Jerry's factory. I met one of the flavor alchemists who was working on, of all flavors, Jalepeno Ice. When I told him about my addiction he said, "Be careful. I pedaled out here from the west coast five years ago." Before we parted, he showed me a bin where the factory sold its "seconds" for a buck—pints that had too much chocolate, for example, or too many nuts and therefore didn't pass inspection. I sat down on the porch with a big spoon and polished off three within the hour, while all the time wondering how I could attach a cooler to my bike and buy out the remaining stock.

The critical role ice cream played in my diet as a cyclist was never more pronounced than in India ... where I couldn't find any. Refrigeration is an absolute luxury, so ice cream does not exist except in the largest of cities. I tried to make up the calories with other desserts, but (and I never thought this was possible) the desserts were all too sweet. They made my teeth ache and my eyes roll back in my head. Without ice cream to buoy my body weight, I dropped twenty pounds. This condition would delight most people, but I had been skinny when I left for India!

My addictive splurges peaked in Canada. It seemed that every town in every eastern province had its own dairy and brand of ice cream and I had to try them all. The long summer days of pedaling just meant that many more hours in which to consume frozen delights.

I pulled into a store in Ontario that had a tell-tale ice cream cone cardboard cutout. I noticed that the woman behind the counter had an enormous right forearm (the sign of a world-class scooper). I ordered a triple (including something called "moose droppings") and was rewarded with at least a quart of ice cream balanced on a sugar cone.

In honor of Uncle Joe, I ordered another. The woman didn't even look surprised. But when I came back a third time and ordered two scoops "to go" she said, "Honey. In all my years of serving ice cream, nobody has ever come back for thirds. This one's on the house."

There were entire days where I ate nothing, absolutely nothing, other than ice cream. So when my tally of expenses proved that seventeen percent of my budget had been consumed by my addiction, the only thing that surprised me was that the percentage hadn't been higher.

I remember teasing my brother (who is seven years my elder) when he began to put on a few extra pounds. He took my gibes with good-natured humor, but always had a confident look in his eye that said, "Your day will come, little brother."

Well, the free ride of indulgence is over. There is undisputed evidence (unless somehow *all* of my pants were simultaneously shrunk in the drier) that I am expanding. No matter how much I pedal, some of the fourteen percent butter fat clings to my middle. Gone are the days when the only reason to turn down an ice cream cone was because I was already eating one.

I must now learn to walk past the ice cream freezer section and reach for the cartons of lowfat yogurt and nonfat cottage cheese. To nibble on carrots and stalks of broccoli while perusing my bicycle route.

Who am I trying to kid? The *real* reason most cyclists wear lycra shorts is that convenient expandable waistband!

Here's to you, Uncle Joe. I'll raise my next triple scoop to you.

THIN RED LINES

OPEN UP ANY country, state or county road map and you'll find the different categories of roads listed in the key. Languages vary drastically from continent to continent, but the language of maps is pretty universal. Fat red or double red lines represent major highways and thoroughfares. As a cyclist, these are to be avoided at all costs. Lots of concrete, traffic and road kill. Secondary roads are usually solid red or blue lines. These are bread-and-butter bicycle roads; paved, but with less traffic, they wander instead of cutting through the land.

But the more I travel, the more I am drawn to the thin red lines. Fortunately, so is Kat. These are unpaved roads and "other roads," that cover everything from two-lane gravel highways to goat paths. If you follow these red lines, you just don't know what you're gonna find.

On our map of Cuba, a thin red line hugged the coast to the old fortress of Castillo de Jagua.

Perfect.

And just as our map had indicated, the pavement ended at Playa Girón, the scene of the ill-fated, CIA-backed "Bay of Pigs" invasion of Cuba back in 1961. The year I was born.

We stopped at a beach-side bar and ordered a couple of mojitos. I asked the barkeep if it felt strange to serve a United States citizen here, given the history of the place. He looked at Kat and me and said, "No problem. We are all Americans after all, aren't we?"

We laughed and admitted to the young man that Cuba hadn't been on our travel list. We were drawn to it by the simple fact that our government declared we couldn't go.

Playa Girón was the end of the line for the tourist busses. They would return to Havana or the tourist resorts of Varadero. We easily slipped our tandem mountain bike through the small opening of the gate at the edge of the pavement.

The bumpy, sometimes sandy road edged along the turquoise waters of the Caribbean. We stopped at a small bay and shared oranges and rum with some local fishermen. No need to hurry on this thin red line.

The road narrowed and edged a bit inland. We passed through a village where *carboneros* still make charcoal from mangrove branches in large earthen ovens.

Several miles down the road we found a flat, but rocky patch of beach and slept out under the stars and a gibbous moon.

In the morning the road narrowed even further. Thorny trees and bushes often plucked our caps from our heads. We stopped to fix a flat on our tandem mountain bike and were treated to the serenades of parrots and tanagers.

And then without sign or warning our coastal road ended. I gazed at our map. The thin red line spanned the coast, unbroken, connecting up with our destination. I looked up and saw a barren, rocky coast. No road. Not even a path. As much as I like to explore the roads represented by fine squiggly lines, they often lead to dead-ends, swamps, or impassable spans where bridges once stood.

Let's face it. Cartographers have to work within a budget, like most of the rest of us. You plot out the major highways and secondary roads, and, if you have time and money you get around to mapping out and authenticating those thin red lines.

I can hear the conversation now.

"Hey Charlie. Does this road continue all the way along the coast?"

"I don't know. But we go to press tomorrow, just draw it in. Nobody travels that stretch of road anyway."

Nobody but a few locals and an occasional adventure cyclist. Our only option was to turn north and head inland.

The path soon opened up into a grid of wide concrete roads and we were cycling in a maze of large warehouses. Cranes and rusting equipment lay scattered about. The streets were eerily quiet. We passed piles of re-bar, steel girders and chunks of broken concrete. Then around a corner we caught sight of an enormous concrete dome looming in the blue sky distance. We somehow had managed to wander into the middle of a nuclear power plant complex.

"We shouldn't be here," we communicated without uttering a word.

There was panic and a scramble to try and retrace our tracks, but an armed guard discovered us before we discovered the exit.

He spoke into his radio and it blared back at him. He motioned for us to follow and escorted us down to the next block, where we were passed off to another machine-gun-toting guard.

By the time a truck pulled up and four more armed guards piled out to assist in the escort, I could see the newspaper headline: "Two U.S. Spies Posing as Cycle Tourists Sentenced to Life in Prison."

This was going to get ugly fast, and Jesse Jackson and Jimmy Carter were no doubt going to have to be involved in negotiating our release.

At the main gate, enclosed by razor wire and large signs stating, "*Prohibido,*" we were presented to the head of operations. We smiled and tried to make small talk to mask our fear. While he studied our passports, I pointed to our map and tried to explain that although we were presently surrounded by barbed-wire, that our entrance had been devoid of gates or "No Trespassing" signs, which I fear came out in my nervously poor Spanish as, "No big pieces of wood. We not bad."

As daunting as this situation appeared, after the head of operations disappeared with our passports, a few of the guards brought us some folding chairs and offered us a couple of bottles of soda.

Several armed men gathered around, admiring our fully loaded tandem mountain bike. At the airport in Havana, the taxi drivers had christened it, *El Tren* (The Train).

Cubans had not always been so interested in bicycles. But when the Soviet Union collapsed and oil became scarce overnight on the island, desperate measures were needed. Over the next couple of years, Fidel Castro imported 1.5 million single-speed Chinese bicycles, and Cubans got a crash course on being a cycling culture. In today's Cuba, if you sit on a balcony in the town square of any major town or city, bicycles will outnumber cars thirty to one.

Several sodas later, the commander appeared with a verdict. We had breached national security, but only a little bit. We had had the good fortune to wander onto a non-functioning nuclear power plant. Construction had ended in 1992 when funding dried up after the collapse of the Soviet Union. These poor, bored military personal were in charge of guarding a nuclear reactor that had never reacted.

After signing a few documents, we were released from custody and escorted out to the main road. Several of the guards smiled and waved as we pedaled off. It wasn't until we were far beyond the gate that I managed to let out a sigh of relief.

Looking back at the nuclear reactor's unfinished cooling tower, we nervously laughed and promised ourselves that we'd stick to the main and secondary roads from then on.

But we both knew it wouldn't be long until the lure of thin red lines made liars of us both.

ARMANDITO'S

Cows MOOED IN low drones, chickens clucked and scratched, cats paced with fixed attention to rats scurrying in the rafters overhead. And the pigs—the pigs squealed and grunted, occasionally blowing bubbles in their slop.

I glanced at my watch. It was 3 AM!

I'd always heard about the peace and tranquility of life in the country. And being a city slicker all of my life, I believed these tales. But the combined din of the barnyard animals at least equaled that of the Boeing jets that fly over our home in Seattle.

The only ones sleeping through this night were our hosts—Armandito and his wife, both snoring away.

We met Armandito at a roadside coffee stand in the little town of outside of Camaguey, Cuba. We were looking for a place to stay, but the locals said there wasn't a hotel and that we'd have to keep moving.

Armandito overheard our conversation and said he'd ask around to see if someone would take us in. He added that he'd offer his place, but he lived out in the country.

"How far?" I asked.

"About six kilometers."

"Could we bicycle out there?"

His eyes lit up and his handsome smile deepened the wrinkles around his intense eyes. He took the cigar out of his mouth.

"You mean you'd like to stay on my farm?"

From that moment, Armandito became the grandest host a pair of travelers could ever hope for.

We all pedaled out to the farm, Kat and I on our tandem and Armandito, clanking and rattling on his single speed, Chinese made "Flying Pigeon" with bald tires. We arrived as the sunset's golden light was just beginning to fade.

If you are picturing a scene in the country with a large farmhouse with a white picket fence and a red barn out back, let me revise your vision.

The one-room farmhouse had bare earth floors, no electricity, no plumbing, no running water, no phone. There was no barn. You could reach out and touch the twenty-five head of dairy cattle from your bedside. More like living in a duplex with farm animals as roommates.

But the conditions didn't matter, because Armandito was so filled with life and intensity and treated us with such graciousness, that this little broken-down farmhouse became a palace on a grand estate.

At around 6 AM, after managing to have slept an hour, I wandered outside to find Armandito, yesterday's cigar clenched in his teeth, his cheek pressed up against the belly of one of his dairy cows, busy milking away.

He stood up to greet me and gestured out at the pasture covered in a blanket of mist and said the Spanish equivalent of "Ain't life grand!"

After all the cows had been milked and we had all washed up, we sat down to a breakfast of milk mixed with fresh-squeezed orange juice, sweet brown bread and farmer's cheese, aged all of twelve minutes, so fresh it squeaked as we chewed it.

Armandito's youngest son, Junior, took us on a horseback ride around the farm. Not far from the house we discovered why we hadn't been able to sleep. Thieves had come in the middle of the night and butchered one of their bulls. There was nothing left but a pile of bones. The animals had been screaming bloody murder all night long, but the humans hadn't listened.

As terrible as this loss was, Armandito refused to let it spoil the visit of his guests. He would later need to file a long report with police to protect himself. Any slaughtering of cattle is a crime, and selling meat on the black market carries up to a fifteen-year prison term. All beef must be sold through the state.

Armandito walked us through his fields. He was proud of the many different crops they grew, everything from sugar cane to yucca to plantains. College-educated with a degree in nutrition, not only did he point out his crops, but he also listed the nutrients in each.

While Cubans living in cities have been hard-hit by the blockade and bad economic times, life hasn't changed much for Armandito and family. They've never had much, but they've always had enough.

We spent two days on the farm, filled with visits from his sons and their families, walks in the countryside and all the squeaky cheese we could eat. All the animals slept soundly the following night, as did we.

In the morning we packed up our bike, one pannier filled with gifts of oranges and grapefruits and cheese. Surrounded by his family, Armandito gave us each bear hugs and wished us well. I smiled back at a man who was a stranger a matter of days ago and shook his cal-lused farm hand with my city-smooth one.

In that moment Cuba came alive to me. It was no longer a vague collection of policies, news clips and sound bites. For I had felt Cuba in a farmer's embrace and seen it through Armandito's eyes.

BUYING TIME

I WAS A thirty-six year-old adventure cyclist facing one of my biggest fears. "The Big M." A Mortgage ... as in thirty-year!

It was always my belief that if I so much as put my toe into the Olympic-sized pool of debt that comes with home ownership, my traveling days would be over. A mortgage was a burden that would weigh down my lifestyle—the equivalent of trying to cycle up a mountain pass with my panniers loaded with bowling balls.

Kat and I realized, with the housing market the way it was in Seattle, that we needed to buy a house, or face having to leave the city as rents skyrocketed. Buying a house went against every fiber in my traveling body. I had managed to bicycle the world, often in five-month stretches, without ever having made over poverty wages in my life. I never had much money, but what I did have was time.

In our consumer culture, time is undervalued. From the moment we are old enough to watch cartoons on TV, we are bombarded with ads to sell us things. In the good old U.S.A. it seems you can never have enough stuff, but you can have "too much time on your hands."

For me, time is one of the essential elements of adventure. Would we have learned about Columbus' voyage in school if it had only taken him four days to sail to the New World? Would authors still be penning books about Lewis and Clark if their expedition had spanned a weekend? I think not.

I learned my own "time vs. money" lesson as a bicycle tour guide. For four years I worked from summer to fall, leading bike trips along the Oregon Coast and throughout the San Juan Islands of Washington. Rather than rent an apartment for those days I was not on the road, I got creative. For fifty dollars a month, my buddy and fellow-guide, Leo, and I, rented a garage. Not a garage converted into bedroom, just a concrete pad with a roof over it and a rusty mower parked in the corner. The nearest bathroom was at the local park.

Many would call this approach extreme. But in my opinion, so is working fifty to seventy hours a week at a job you hate in order to pay off a brand new Range Rover or interest on credit card debt. Yes, having to walk several blocks to use the john was annoying, but I was ecstatic with my living arrangement. For with every dollar I saved, I was buying time. More time on the road. More mountain passes to climb. Deserts to cross. Exotic lands, food and people to discover.

While on the job as a tour guide, it was ironic to be surrounded by guests who had paid more money to be guided on an eight-day custom bicycle trip than I would spend in five months on the road. As we sat around the tables at fine restaurants, trying to make up our minds between salmon or halibut, I listened to the stories of extremely successful people. Most of them made more money in a month than I would make in a year. But they envied my lifestyle.

After six to eight magical days it was back to "reality," as many of them called their jobs. Every one of them had enough money to travel the world several times over, but most were bankrupt of free time.

As soon as the tourist season was over I was off on my own bicycle adventures. Each year I would return to my garage/apartment with little money in the bank, but an invaluable cache of travel memories.

I had always thought the only way I could maintain my adventure lifestyle was by remaining single and sleeping on garage floors. If I entered the mainstream it would all be over.

So years later, finding myself married and sitting in a real estate agent's office, there was every reason to believe I would soon be a homebody. It didn't help that Seattle's real-estate market had defied national averages. While housing prices had remained flat for several years around most of the country, homes in Seattle had rocketed up twenty to forty-five percent. I was about to trade in my panniers for payments—360 of them.

Then a miracle happened.

When the real estate agent asked us what we were looking for Kat immediately responded, "Small and ugly."

The woman looked at her with surprise. "I'm not sure I hear you correctly. What are you looking for?"

"Small and ugly," Kat repeated. "That's what we can afford, so why look at the others? If we buy anything beyond that, it is going to be a long time before we leave on another bike trip." Kat looked at me and smiled.

My traveler's heart soared. Wow. I had married the right woman!

With Kat's response my mortgage fears melted away. We had agreed that if we wanted to make bicycle travel a priority, we needed to make the life and financial choices to allow it to happen. She had put our discussions into action.

Four days later we put in an offer on a house.

Yes, it was small. Yes, it was ugly. The prior owners had done us the favor of painting the house bright turquoise. We swore that they paid a crop duster to paint the house, as they had managed to coat not only the house in turquoise paint, but the fence, sidewalk and even the shrubs. It had only had one (horrors!) bathroom. But it also had a feature that was irresistible. It had a price low enough that we didn't have to work fifty weeks out of the year in order to eke out our monthly payments. We dubbed it The Turquoise Palace.

With the decision to purchase "small and ugly", we bought ourselves time. And there is nothing like packing for a three-month bicycle trip to transform a small and ugly house into a palace.

THE LANGUAGE BARRIER

FOREIGN LANGUAGE. THOSE two words keep many travelers from living out their dreams. I can't tell you how many times I have heard die-hard travel enthusiasts use the inability to speak the local language as an excuse to avoid much of the globe. They have the money. They have the time. They just don't have a handle on the language. And once they become proficient in French or German or Hindi or Swahili, they will take that trip of a lifetime.

Don't hesitate. Go now! Even if you don't know a single word of your dream country's language.

"Oh, but Willie," I hear you say. "You have cycled all over the world and obviously have a knack for languages. It's not that easy for most of us."

Well, you're wrong. I'm horrible with languages. I barely passed Spanish in high school. I hated it. I sat in the back of the class (near the door for a quick exit) and prayed that my teacher wouldn't call on me.

But he did.

"Luis," he would begin. (That was my given Spanish name. There was another William in the class, so Guillermo had already been taken). Then he would proceed to ask me a question in Spanish.

My response was always the same: "*Lo siento. No se.*" (I'm sorry. I don't know.)

At least that is what I verbalized. What I was saying internally was, "Could you please give me a break? I'm only taking this class because I need two years of a foreign language in order to go to college. I'm going to major in biology and go count birds in a national park somewhere or study the eating habits of badgers."

"I don't need to speak a foreign language. I don't want to travel to Mexico or Spain. I just want to correctly conjugate the minimum number of verbs in order to get a C in this miserable class of yours and move on with my life, thank you very much."

I managed a C and barely a C- in my second year of torture. I had fulfilled my foreign language requirement and no one would ever make me speak a foreign language again.

The irony was not lost on me when, ten years later, I assembled my bicycle in the San Diego Amtrak station, the starting point for a solo bicycle journey throughout Mexico.

I had cycled across the United States and Canada and had dreams and plans to pedal Ireland, Scotland, Australia, New Zealand, England and Wales. But I thought I'd warm-up with a ride across the southern United States. I had feebly tried to convince myself that these were the countries I most longed to visit. But late one sleepless evening, I had to admit to myself that I was scared to travel in a country where English was not the predominant language.

This language barrier (as large and looming as the Great Wall of China) stood between me and a world of travel opportunities.

It was time to face my fear and have an adventure. Instead of traveling east from San Diego, I pedaled south and soon crossed the border into Mexico.

My first encounter was with a local policeman in Tijuana who asked me something about my bicycle ... I think. I responded with, "*Lo siento. No se.*" He smiled, quite content with my answer.

Within two days my entire view of the world changed. My Spanish still sucked, but I managed to communicate. Not a single person asked me to conjugate a verb. Within one week I could understand and speak more Spanish than I could after two years of classes.

And when I butchered a phrase at the market or in a restaurant, I was always rewarded with enormous smiles from locals, just for having tried to speak their language. I had been a C- student, but I was an A+ traveler.

My bicycle journey through Mexico was such a rewarding experience that I spent three months cycling Central America the following year. By the time I reached Panama, my language barrier had been reduced to a language speed bump.

Along the way I had learned that you do not need to know a single word of a foreign language to have a grand adventure. That's right. In fact, many of my favorite travel memories are experiences where no conversations took place.

In the mountains of Chiapas, Mexico, I was taken in by a family who spoke no Spanish. Their language was a Mayan dialect. The father and I spent the late evening together gazing up at a cloudless sky littered with stars. I pointed up to a constellation and gave him the English name and he in return taught me the Mayan equivalent.

In a small village in Rajastan, India, a family invited me into their crude stone dwelling. We shared food. We danced. We drank. I met the local dignitaries ... not a word was spoken.

In Romania, Kat and I were setting up our tent near the road when a couple appeared out of the woods. To this day we don't know their names. We refer to them as "the couple of the long limbs" because they were both tall and slender with striking features and workers' hands. With smiles and gestures they led us to their cottage in the woods and fed us a glorious meal. We sat around the table late into the evening, drinking brandy and pantomiming our life stories to each other.

Do you know what I've found more valuable than a phrase book? Juggling balls. That's right—juggling balls. Juggling allows me to make a contribution without saying a word. No matter what part of the globe I find myself on, juggling allows me to make a child smile.

I have met travelers who carry an instrument, who do magic tricks. One German cyclist I met in Mexico traveled with a basketball strapped to his back rack, ready for a game of one-on-one. Your advantage over the typical world traveler is your bike. People will delight in it. Children will swoon over it. Let's face it. A fully loaded touring bike is a better social icebreaker than witty conversation any day.

For those who have a knack for languages … this advice obviously isn't for you. Learn Russian and then go travel Russia. I envy you. Oh, how I envy you.

But like many folks out there, my language aptitude is abysmal. Sure, my experiences might have been richer had I known Mayan and Hindi and Romanian. But if I had waited until I learned those languages before I left, I would have died of old age without seeing the places where they are spoken.

Take this advice. Forget the years of language school and audio-tapes. Pick a country. Learn how to say "Hello" and "Thank you" and "How much?" and learn to count to ten. Then pack your bicycle or your backpack and go.

Do you dream of cycling in a foreign land? Remember, the language barrier is only as tall and wide as you make it.

BALDWIN STREET

CLIMBING MOUNTAIN PASSES and steep hills on a bicycle (especially a fully-loaded one) is surely a daunting task. Lots of training will help, but I've never been very disciplined. I've always looked for shortcuts.

I have discovered that if I push my body to its extreme, then everything else seems easy in comparison. Mountain passes always made me nervous and anxious. So (with very little training) I went out and rode the Markleeville Death Ride (an insane one-day 150-mile ride over the five major mountain passes of the Sierras). That did it. Afterwards, no single mountain pass felt remotely daunting.

Now I realize that this is not an intelligent strategy. It is akin to suggesting to a carpenter that he smash his hand with a sledge hammer so that in the future when he misses a nail with his framing hammer and connects with his thumb, it will feel good in comparison. But it works for me.

Hills, rather than mountain passes, have always been even more of a mental challenge for me. Hills are just plain unfair: little, tiny annoying mountain passes, with no summit signs and rarely a rewarding view from the top. Nothing psyched me out more than an endless day of hills, until Baldwin Street.

On the east coast of the South Island of New Zealand lies the city of Dunedin. It is known as the Edinburgh of the Southern

Hemisphere. Mark Twain described it best: "Many Scots stopped in Dunedin on the way to heaven, thinking they had arrived."

My bicycle wanderings around "the isle of the long cloud" brought me into this fair city not long after the summer solstice (December 21). I bellied up to the bar at a tavern on one of the main streets. The barkeep, a man in his fifties with a barrel chest and thick, long eyebrows that stuck out like awnings on a craftsman home, poured me a pint.

"Are you a cyclist, or do ya just like wearing those funny shorts?" he asked as he wiped up a dribble of porter from his shiny bar counter.

I told him that I was in the midst of a four-month pedaling journey around his picture perfect country.

He leaned close. "So you're from the good ol' U.S. of A? Tell me this. Do you know where the steepest street in the world is?"

I could see by his grin that this was a leading question. His eyebrows arched up toward the ceiling, awaiting my response.

"San Francisco would be my guess," stating the obvious.

He slapped the bar counter with his meaty hand, "You're wrong. Off by half the distance of the globe." He shook out his towel and his voice rose up. "In this, the fairest city in the fairest country on God's green earth, lies the world's steepest street. Baldwin Street is its name. Check it out for yourself in that Guinness Book. Or better yet, go have yourself a bit of a pedal up it. If you dare to."

Now I'm not one to run off and do just anything on a dare. But if Baldwin Street was the steepest street on the planet, when would I ever have another chance to climb it?

After a restless night filled with steep gradient dreams, I woke up early the next morning at the Dunedin youth hostel with nothing but Baldwin Street on my mind.

Baseball players warm up by swinging their bats in the on-deck circle. Some swing three or four bats, others attach a heavy metal donut to the end of their own bat. Just before they walk up to the plate, they drop the extra weight, which gives the sensation that their Louisville Slugger is now as light as air. I did the touring cyclist's equivalent.

I unloaded all my gear: my tent, sleeping bag, sleeping mattress, lock, spare parts, spare tire, the jar of spaghetti sauce I had bought a week prior, an internal frame backpack I had stuffed in a compression sack, T-shirts, socks, cooking pot, two travel guides, stove, sweats, shampoo, twelve rolls of film, dental floss ... it was all left behind. I felt like a bird.

Baldwin Street is just a wee bit north of the center of downtown Dunedin. I flew down the city streets, following the directions someone at the hostel had given me. Climbing the steep streets of Seattle for many years had prepared me for just this occasion. This was going to be fun.

I whipped around a corner and came upon the infamous street. There was no mistaking it. "Oh, ... my ... God," I whispered in awe.

All the energy stored up in my legs drained out in a matter of seconds and every molecule in my body screamed, "You can't do this! You won't do this."

I glanced up at two signs—A large yellow traffic diamond with a single exclamation point and a black bordered sign below that read, "For Safety Reasons: Sightseers are requested not to drive up this street." It unfortunately mentioned nothing about pedaling.

Filbert Street and 22nd Street are the steepest streets in San Francisco. Both have a maximum gradient of 1 in 1.853 (28.35° or 31%) which makes them popular with tourists, triathletes and movie companies (who like to shoot cars over them at insane speeds, leading us to believe that every San Francisco city cop spends half his or her day airborne). Tourists and locals all just assume that nowhere could streets be steeper.

Yet in humble little Dunedin, on the South Island of New Zealand, Baldwin Street peaks at a maximum gradient of 1 in 1.266 (38° or 42.2%)!

I shifted into first gear to save having to do so under stress, and began my ascent. My goal was to just keep on pedaling until I fell over (due to gravity or a heart attack). The Guinness-breaking grade was about two-thirds up the hill, so I had some time to warm up before failing miserably.

My legs obediently pumped away and I quickly had to stand as the grade increased. As I hit the steepest section, I began to grunt and yell with every exhalation.

No way. My body just wasn't up to this.

Then I heard some clapping and yelling and glanced up to see a family of Japanese tourists cheering me on. The two younger kids jumped up and down and pumped their fists. A surge of adrenaline cursed through my body and I leaned forward and attempted to touch my nose to the front tire. My tires began to slip and I came to a brief halt, clumsily balanced, my front tire a half of an inch off the pavement. With one last groan, my back tire grabbed the hill and I felt my body begin to straighten up. To the sounds of whopping and hollering and several congratulatory Japanese phrases, I sprinted up the last section of the hill.

For the next several minutes, I could feel my heart pounding in my chest, my head, my groin, even my feet. I had managed to pedal up the steepest street on earth.

The feeling of euphoria was brief, and I have to be honest and admit that the view looking down a 42.2 percent grade was so terrifying that I opted to slowly walk my bike back to the level street below.

But the true rewards of that climb continue to be reaped today. Because every time I reach a hill that pulls me out of my saddle, I have a mantra that works wonders … "It ain't as steep as Baldwin Street. It ain't as steep as Baldwin Street. It ain't …"

INITIATING KINDNESS

MY FRIEND RANDY joined me for a couple of weeks of cycling on the South Island during my five month journey throughout New Zealand.

Randy had heard hundreds of my stories about past adventures—how I avoided campgrounds whenever possible, preferring to knock on a door at the end of the day's travels, and how these encounters often led to home-cooked meals and soft feather beds.

Randy had a term for my style. He called it "mooching" or "freeloading." I preferred my own term, a pet theory, fashioned from years of travel and observance— "initiating kindness".

Before you laugh as Randy always did, let me explain.

You see, I believe that most people want to be kind. But today's fast-paced, paranoid, litigation-driven society has robbed them of most opportunities. You don't pull over to help someone who is having car trouble. You call 911 on your cell phone instead.

You don't give spare change to the man or woman with the cup and the "No food. No work" sign. You send a check to a food bank.

If someone knocks on your door and asks to use the phone, you give them directions to the nearest pay phone, because prime time television has convinced you that most strangers are on the FBI's most wanted list.

Enter the touring cyclist, the last of a dying breed. When we ask for water or directions or for a place to set up our tents, we initiate kindness. Because of the inherent vulnerable and innocent qualities that a bicycle projects, people are able to get past all the warnings our society has heaped on them about thieves, rapists and mass murderers. They can reach out and be kind to a fellow human being, beyond sending a check to a nonprofit organization, and that makes them feel good.

I used to feel guilty that people where housing and feeding me without getting anything in return. Then one morning in upstate New York I was thanking a family who had taken me into their home and out of some severe thunderstorms. The mother gave me a big hug and said, "No. It is I who need to thank you. For the first time in years, I am going to go to the office today and have something exciting to talk about."

People love to vicariously be part of an adventure. It brings excitement into the routine. It is the very reason that many a touring cyclist who is not on the road, pulls over anyone with a bike and panniers and insists on helping them somehow. If we can't be on our own adventure, being part of somebody else's is the next best thing.

I know that the boy scouts motto is "be prepared", but I say the traveling cyclist's motto should be "don't be too prepared". You can't be an initiator of kindness if you travel with panniers stuffed with energy bars, enough spare parts to stock a mid-sized repair shop, and nightly reservations at campgrounds or hotels.

I have come to see myself as an ambassador as well as a traveler. A random "initiator of kindness".

It's hard to explain this to anyone who hasn't been out cycling on the open road for months at a time.

Randy had heard all about my theory, but still called me "The World's Greatest Mooch". We agreed that we would camp at campgrounds if they were available, but if the situation called for it, he would be willing to knock on a door or two.

Late in the evening of our first day of pedaling we pulled into a pub. After eating a few mutton sandwiches and playing a game of darts, we cycled through town, wondering where we could stay. I spied a Catholic church down one block. The architecture wasn't unique, but the color was—bright purple.

"Hey, Randy. Let's go initiate some kindness."

He rolled his eyes, but gave the go ahead.

I knocked on the door of the church and was greeted by Father Leo. When I asked him if we could pitch our tents on church property, he said he could do us one better and offer us beds for the night.

Father Leo was quite a character, and kept us up late telling us stories about the townsfolk and explaining the rules of cricket. Before we went to bed he answered my burning question.

"We got the paint on sale. It was supposed to be pale blue. But it dried purple. We don't have any more money in the restoration budget, so purple it will remain. It kind of grows on you."

The next morning after hardy bowls of oatmeal, Father Leo walked us out to our bikes.

"Thank you, lads, for stopping in. Between Sundays it can get lonesome here. God bless you."

The next evening we decided to camp. Campgrounds in New Zealand are plush by U.S. standards, with manicured grounds, clean bathrooms with large showers, and kitchen blocks with stoves and sinks for all to share.

Our perfectly flat site had a view of the lake. We went down to a field and watched some locals play "touch sevens", a less brutal form of rugby. We returned and ate ramen noodles with vegetables. We were surrounded by dozens of travelers, yet no one said a word to us. Everyone was busy with his or her own travel agenda.

We quietly pulled out of our campsite in the early morning and pedaled toward our first New Zealand mountain pass. The views were spectacular and it was fun to watch Randy reach his first summit on a fully loaded mountain bike. We had been friends since high school, but our busy lives rarely gave us time to spend with one another anymore. We pedaled hour after hour, talking of anything and everything.

We stopped and asked for water at one farm and ended up eating lunch with rock pickers and musterers. A man named Ross and his friend had been working a piece of land, removing the rocks so it could be planted (rock pickers). The rest of the lads were musterers—called that because they muster up the sheep from the fields, with the help of well-trained sheepdogs, for shearing, dipping, tailing and weaning.

They all thought the roads in New Zealand were too crowded. We tried to explain LA and the traffic there. "Now picture every sheep as a car ... "

We departed after filling our bellies with lamb, potatoes, carrots and bread pudding.

Pedaling slowly down the highway, we waited for our feast to digest. We hadn't discussed where we'd sleep that evening. I wasn't too keen about spending the remainder of our nights in campgrounds, but I was willing to do whatever made Randy the most comfortable.

Late in the afternoon I finally asked, "Randy. So what will it be tonight, camping or knocking?"

Randy stopped pedaling and looked at me with a wry smile.

"Let's initiate some kindness."

WITHOUT A TRACE

I'LL ADMIT IT. I'm spoiled. If I'm going to plan and execute a bicycle journey, it had better be three months or more, or I'd rather not bother.

Every self-contained tour I have ventured on in the last two decades has been nintey days or longer. Hey. If I'm going to cancel my newspaper and put my mail on hold I might as well put my stuff in storage, and make a long journey of it.

Of course "long" is a relative term. To some of the folks I have met on the road, three months is just the beginning—a warm-up. I met a Polish cyclist in Central America who had been on the road for eight years. He had a permanent sunburn and that crazed look of a shipwreck survivor. He was traveling with three large pineapples strapped to his rack and an even larger machete strapped to the front rack. He had been around the world three times. When I asked him when he planned to return home, he shook his head and spun his finger in a circle, indicating he had a couple revolutions of the earth in him before he settled back into a "normal" life.

In 1999, Kat and I looked at our schedules and our bank account, and realized we would only be able to swing a nine-day bike tour. Nine days. That was ten percent of my minimum! But it was still a hundred percent more than no trip, so we started planning.

Planning was foreign to me. When I landed in New Delhi, India in December of '94, the only thing I knew for sure was that I was flying out of the same airport five months later. The rest I left to chance and karma.

· When you have 150 days to play with, it is much easier to let fate and wind direction be your guide. But nine days! We needed a plan. A route. A guaranteed round-trip plane reservation.

Our budget made many of our decisions for us. I had been bumped off a flight (twice!) trying to come back to Seattle from Boston the year before and the air voucher came to $600 bucks. I got on the Web and started to search. I discovered that I could get two round trip tickets to Nashville, Tennessee from Seattle for the total of $598.75. And I had an aunt and uncle and cousin Tom who lived there, so chances were, we wouldn't have to spring for a hotel either. Perfect.

I put out the word and asked where we might cycle in the South. Everyone mentioned the Natchez Trace. The Natchez Trace is a wide two-lane national parkway that winds along the overland route taken by folks who had floated down the Mississippi, long before motorboats and jet skis, and needed a way to get back. It took a long time to walk this trail, which had no sanctioned rest areas with free coffee, and most folks got robbed along the way. I had heard from several people that this was one of the premier bike rides in America. Hundreds and hundreds of miles of lush green belt … and no semis. We could do part of it or all of it and then catch a bus or hitch back to Nashville.

When the time came to leave, we even had a plan to make sure we didn't pay the ridiculous, discriminatory "bicycle fee" most airlines like to slap you with. Our Rodriguez tandem has S and S couplings, so we were able to fit the bike into a regular hard shell case. Kat wore business-like clothing to the airport and wheeled the case into line.

It was plastered with corporate stickers that read, "Display Materials." I positioned myself with all of our panniers and bicycle-related gear far enough behind her in line as to not be confused in any way as her travel partner.

When she got to the check-in counter and the woman asked her what was in the box, she did what any red-blooded cyclist who thinks that the airlines policies towards bicycles are insane … she lied. She said in a clear and unwavering voice … "It contains display materials for a convention I'm attending."

No charge.

Then when the same woman looked at me and all my gear minutes later and asked, "Where is your bicycle?" I said, "It's on display." I couldn't help but give Kat a conspiratorial wink.

Turns out that Uncle Don and Aunt Dot lived less than ten miles from the beginning (or end) of the Trace. After a full breakfast while watching cardinals and grosbeaks out the window, we hopped on our tandem and pedaled through neighborhoods with no fences and lush green yards. Soon we were turning on to the Trace. "Mississippi, here we come."

Although the Natchez Trace is held in high esteem as one of the premier bicycle routes in America, I quickly discovered it was my worst nightmare. Why? Because I knew exactly where I was going. This sent shivers up my spine. We couldn't get lost. Not that I wake up every morning hoping to get lost, but maintaining the possibility of getting lost is essential to my sense of adventure.

I also noted that the Natchez Trace bypassed most towns. The idea of cycling through the South without stopping at dozens of corner stores and bars and town halls depressed me. Sure it was a historic path, but I'm one of those that would rather delve into living history. Call me crazy, but I'd rather have a conversation at a bar with a local about his great grandfather than read plaques and signboards about important battles and dead folks.

I found myself looking longingly at every side road that split off from the Trace. "I wonder where that one leads to …" I didn't think my body language was so apparent, but soon I heard Kat say, "You want to get off this parkway, don't you?"

"Can we?"

She smiled. "It wasn't my idea to cycle the Trace."

We pulled off and got out the map. A small county road snaked off the Trace—a tiny, thin red line.

An old 1950-something Ford pickup came rattling down the road and we waved it down. An old man hopped out of the driver's seat, forgetting to put the truck in park, so one of the passengers had to lurch forward to step on the break to bring the Ford to a complete stop.

We pointed to the road on our map and asked if he could show us the way.

He answered in a thick Tennessee drawl that we could barely make out as English. "Sure as hell can. It's nearby. That's the wiggliest damn road you ever saw."

Kat and I both smiled. Our journey along the Natchez Trace Parkway ended that second. It was off to "who knows where" … our favorite destination.

The old man was right. It was the wiggliest damn road he or we had ever seen. We coasted down the narrow road, farther and farther from our originally planned route. The overhanging trees stretched out and embraced us in a perfectly cool canopy of green.

The road opened and followed a small river. In a matter of minutes, we were far away from any sign of tourists or motor homes, pedaling through small towns I thought no longer existed outside of movies and Civil War documentaries.

We stopped in at a tiny grocery store/gas station. The old 7-up sign was faded to just this side of invisible and the screen door to the store creaked as loud as the laughter of the woman behind the counter telling a joke to a customer. We bought a soda and a couple of Moon Pies and sat out on the porch.

Now that we had spontaneously ditched our plans … where were we going? I spread out our map of Tennessee on the faded wooden planks. North? South? East? West? Which way?

My finger traced along the secondary roads headed west.

"Let's go to Graceland," I blurted out. "Elvis and these wiggly roads are calling our names."

Neither Kat nor I had ever been to this shrine of Rock and Roll. So our new destination became Memphis. Mississippi would have to wait for another trip; we were going to see The King.

We pedaled on into the heat of mid-afternoon through a valley settled by Mennonites. Each farm had dozens of gourds strung between trees to house the South's best bug control, purple martins.

"Couldn't help but notice your tandem out there. Where are you headed?"

The questioner was a stocky man with long hair and a substantial salt-and-pepper beard who approached us in a local organic vegetable market.

We explained our plans to pedal to Graceland.

"Where you staying tonight?"

No plans, we told him.

"I got an old shingle shack out on my property you are welcomed to."

I smiled. Not much had changed in eighteen years since my first cross-country tour. "We'll take you up on it."

Our host described himself as a Harley Davidson-ridin', ten-dollar preacher.

"Is that how much you charge?" I asked.

"No," he said with a huge grin. "That's how much it cost to get ordained."

Our modest accommodations were near a babbling brook on a couple of idyllic country acres far off the main highway.

"It doesn't have plumbing or electricity, but you'll have plenty of privacy. I'm going into town to stay with my grandson. I'll check up on you in the morning."

The next day we pedaled into the Shilo National Park. We wandered about the old battlefields and did yoga on the expansive green lawn outside the visitor center. Yoga is obviously not practiced with regularity in the Southern United States because several times we heard, "Hey Mom. What are those funny people doing?"

The state highway headed west offered us a smooth, peaceful Sunday evening's ride ... until about 5:30 PM, when everyone with a truck and a boat who'd escaped the city of Memphis for the weekend, decided to get back—in a hurry. Hundreds of Fords, Chevys and GMs screamed closely by us dragging their loud weekend flotilla of fishing boats, speed boats and monster jet skis.

"We've got to get off the road, now!," I yelled back to Kat.

There was no campground in site or on our map, so I suggested we knock on a door. There were several houses along the highway. Kat asked, "I know you have always been one to feel free to knock on a door in this type of situation. But how do you know which one?"

"I don't know for sure," I said. "Sometimes it's the garden. I've always figured that if people are nice to plants, they'll be nice to humans as well. Sometimes it is just a feeling."

I pointed to a simple white house with a carport. "I don't know why, but that one gives me good vibes."

A woman peered out at us through the bars of her screen door. I noticed bars on the windows as well. Not a good sign. Perhaps I had lost my touch.

We explained to the woman that we were simply looking for a place to pitch a tent. She hesitated till she saw our tandem and pointed out back.

Her property opened up to a lush green field and a lake. It was, quite frankly, the most beautiful campsite I've ever pitched a tent on.

We didn't expect to see our hostess that evening. But Francis wandered out to see that we were settled, and soon invited us for some iced-tea on her patio.

"As long as the purple martins are out, we're fine. But once they go to bed, we'll be eaten alive out here."

Before the mosquitoes descended upon us, she invited us in for some cake and conversation.

A tiny, spunky woman in her seventies, she told us stories from her childhood. She pointed to the house she grew up in up on the hill. She was the oldest of three girls, and loved to play practical jokes. Her daddy was a good man, but didn't have much of a sense of humor. One day she took her daddy's best pair of boots and painted them bright red. He came home from work and put them on.

"He never said a word. Never. Took all the fun out of it," she chuckled.

When we asked her what the most important invention was during her lifetime? Without a moment's hesitation came her reply, "Air conditioning!"

Francis had worked out of her home as a beautician for thirty-five years, making her house the center of news and gossip for the county. Perhaps that is the reason she was deputized by none other than Buford Pusser himself, the Tennessee sheriff who became a legend even before three "Walking Tall" movies were made about his life.

She put on a devilish grin and said, "Buford once told me, 'Francis. If you ever see anyone suspicious hanging around your place, shoot'em, drag'em by the hair into your beauty parlor, then give me a call.'"

Late into the evening, we heard stories of moonshining, mayhem and murder. Not what I had expected when I first looked at this tiny woman through the bars of her screen door.

Two days later we pedaled right up to the gates of Graceland. The prior evening had had its own charm. We'd been invited to the 3,000 acre plantation of an ex-Paris Island Marine Corps drill sergeant and his wife.

I never thought that touring the King's mansion would be anti-climatic, but after evenings with a Harley preacher/biker and a deputized beautician, Elvis would have had to have made a personal appearance to have been in the running.

We couldn't believe the breadth of experiences we'd had in such a short trip. None of them planned. All of them unforgettable.

What would our journey have been like if we'd stayed on The Trace? I can't tell you. But I can tell you that off the beaten path there are adventures and characters to be discovered in this country that rival anything I've encountered around the globe.

LETTER FROM A DITCH

I MET A young man named Paul when I was cycling through Mexico. From his sun-kissed leathery skin to his duct-taped shoes and panniers, he was the picture of a long distance cyclist. He had been on the road for years, having criss-crossed the U.S. a couple of times, then up to Alaska, down the coast to South America. He couldn't make up his mind to go north to New Orleans for Mardi Gras or south to Antigua, Guatemala for the Easter processionals.

"You must have one very large journal" I asked.

He laughed. No, he actually guffawed.

"Who has time to write? It's all up here," he said, tapping his temple. "Going to write a book when I finally get home."

Ten years later, I'm still looking for his book. Now maybe he had trouble finding a publisher. But more than likely he found out the hard way about the human brain's limited capacity for storing travel details, thoughts and emotions.

Cycling is a great way to stay in shape, a fabulous way to see the world. It is not conducive to writing. For example, after a seventy-mile day of fighting gale force head winds, being blown off the road a dozen times, you pull into a state park and instantly are invited to party with Nebraska's only all-Norwegian tuba corps. In this situation you want to: A) Eat. B) Party. C) Sleep. D) Write in your journal. E) All of the above, except for D.

Other travelers have it made. They have a surplus of writing opportunities—long waits in airport lounges, hours, sometimes days sitting in buses, trains and boats. Over the course of a round-the-world adventure they may get fat for lack of exercise, but so do their journals.

I'm going to admit something to you. I hate to write. I would rather do almost anything else … balance my checkbook, mow the lawn, change a rear tire in a cold drizzle. The only class I ever flunked in college was English 1A. I actually selected my major (theatre arts) based on the fact that I wouldn't have to write any term papers.

But on the onset of my first cross-country bicycle tour, I knew I had to keep a journal. I had to somehow capture what I knew was going to be an epic journey. I began promisingly the first evening, filling two pages before dozing off. Within a couple of days I was down to two paragraphs on a good night. And within two weeks my daily entries resembled unlabeled answers to a multiple choice quiz.

8-9-81, 82 miles, Pierre-South Dakota, church yard.

Much of that journey is lost to me. I can no longer crack the code.

So I learned my lesson, right? Wrong. I did buy a new and larger journal for my next journey in anticipation of the John Steinbeck emerging in me, and my thoughtful entries filled pages—for almost a week. Then attrition and long hard days set in and I missed a couple of entries. Then the vicious cycle began as I irrationally refused to write about anything currently happening until I caught up. I'd sit crouched over in my tent after an incredibly exciting day feebly trying to remember the events of eleven days prior. Then I would slump into my sleeping bag having written nary a word.

Then my brother came to the rescue.

Jeff is seven years my elder and I love him dearly.

I'm the traveler. He's the unabashed homebody. We both revel in our roles. Part of my frustration about trying to keep a journal on the road was I never seemed to have time to send even a short letter home; I was too busy feeling guilty about *not* writing in my journal.

Then one afternoon I sat in a ditch in Guatemala and penned this:

*I'm hot. I'm tired, and I'm sitting on the side of the road. Ants are feasting on the remains of two oranges I sucked dry. I would have kept going, but the little patch of shade looked as inviting as a swimming pool (with a slide). I **feel** thirty! My bike feels heavy. It is heavy, you fool! As you get older you're supposed to carry less gear, not more. You're supposed to have a tour guide waiting ahead with snacks and cold drinks and kind words. No. I choose to travel unsupported. Carrying the weight of all my possessions and gadgets up each mountain pass. I choose to sit in a ditch and write to my brother while buses speed by, bound for Guatemala City. They'll be there tonight. I'll be lucky if I make it two days from now. But in those two days, I'll learn a little more about myself. I'll appreciate more the food I'll eat, the water I'll drink and the sleep I'll sleep. Oh, how noble can a letter sound written from a ditch.*

I had found my motivation. It was so simple I couldn't believe I hadn't thought of it before. From that moment on I faithfully kept a daily journal … in letters to my brother. They were filled with descriptions and humor and angst and wonder, everything that had been missing from my previous journals. And I never missed a day. Because missing a day meant a day that my brother didn't get to come along on the journey.

Writing went from being a chore that I dreaded to a delightful obligation I couldn't wait to fulfill.

This new approach also reduced excess weight. I've met people on extended trips hauling around journals with more girth than Websters dictionary. I no longer had the need for a bulky bound volume that couldn't fit in my handlebar bag. Each week a new segment went out with the post. When traveling in a country with a less-than-stellar mail service, I'd often photocopy the pages before sending them and keep the copies until I knew the originals had arrived. Journaling via letters also reduced stress. You'll rarely find a more depressed traveler than one who has been robbed and lost his or her painstakingly detailed memories.

Almost a decade has passed since I sat in that ditch in Guatemala, but I can still vividly picture the exact moment I wrote those words. They well up in me scores of emotions and desires for the open road. My mentor, Jim Molnar, a travel columnist for *The Seattle Times* once said to me, "People spend years trying to learn how to honestly express themselves in their writing. You have found that quality through writing to your brother. I'm not one to often give advice, but you should keep those letters coming."

I think it is advice worth passing on. Next time you leave on a journey, why not give it a try. Write to your brother, or your lover, or your mother—whatever and to whomever it takes. Because twenty years from now cryptic notes in a journal won't begin to tell the story.

ITCHING TO TRAVEL

WHAT ABOUT HEALTH issues and diseases? I get that question more than most bicycle travelers. Perhaps it is due to my habit of bicycling in countries and on continents which rarely wind up the "Ten best places to bicycle list"—India, Africa, Bosnia, Albania, Central America. Most people who inquire at the presentations I give around the country want to know which was the worst. In which of these countries did I cry out to the heavens in a feverish trance, begging to be rescued from the living hell I was experiencing.

I look out at the crowd and see expectant faces—young adventurers looking for those places on earth that would test their travel muster, as well as spouses ready to lean over after I've given my answer and whisper, "I told you we should never plan a trip there."

With no need for exhaustive research or the rereading of all my journals, I can matter-of-factly state that Canada wins the prize hands down. Yep. That ominous, mysterious and dangerous country to the north.

It was the spring of 1988 and an announcement for a family reunion dropped onto the floor through the rusty mail slot of my sparsely furnished Seattle apartment. The event was scheduled for early August in upstate New York.

Now most people would head for the newspaper looking for airline deals. But as only avid travelers can truly understand, I saw this as the perfect opportunity (excuse) to take the summer off from my less-than-stellar acting career, cycle all the way across Canada and drop down through the New England states to New York, just in time to party with relatives (most who I'd never met in my life).

I put all of my possessions in a friend's spare closet, gave notice to my nosy, but kind and gentle landlord, and soon pedaled off toward Vancouver, British Columbia.

Everything was rolling along splendidly—long, beautiful days in the saddle, Banff, Jasper, Lake Louise, the Yellowhead Highway through Alberta and the endless wheat fields of Saskatchewan. Then I hit Ontario and black flies. They descended upon me in swarms, clouds, battalions and mobs. The rest of Canada celebrated the bug-less June, for each and every black fly in all eleven provinces was attracted to me. I literally dove into one roadside bar seeking refuge from the onslaught at three in the afternoon. As I wiped the blood off my legs from the scores of bites, I asked the bartender when was the peak of black fly season. He nonchalantly glanced at his watch, and in deadpan delivery answered, "Right about now."

In the following days I began to feel weak. Was it possibly the loss of blood? I stumbled out of my tent at a provincial park, scratching my head, and felt dozens of bumps. How could it be? I'd been wearing a hat AND a helmet. I stumbled into the bathroom and looked in the mirror and gasped. I was covered, head to foot, in red bumps. I pictured the National Inquirer headline, "U.S. Man Dies From Six Million Canadian Black Fly Bites".

I managed to summon up the energy to pedal to the nearest city, Thunder Bay, and found a hospital with an emergency room.

The intern examined me, held his clip board against his chest and said, "I wish I could tell you that you are suffering from something more exotic, but you my friend, have the worst case of chickenpox I've ever seen."

Chickenpox?!

Oh great. My epic bicycle journey across Canada was over. Stopped dead in its tire tracks by a childhood virus. You can tell impressive tales of surviving typhoid in India, sleeping sickness in Africa, malaria in Central America ... but the chickenpox in Canada? That's not adventure, that's comedy.

But let me tell you, in children, chicken pox is normally a nuisance. When it hits you as an adult, it packs a Joe Louis punch that can take months to get over and can leave you sterile to boot.

The question remained, where did I pick-up the chickenpox. The doctor told me the gestation period was about three weeks. I flipped back in my journal and called a childhood friend of mine who had ended up as a pastor in a church in Edmonton, Alberta.

"Hey Steve."

"Willie. Didn't expect to hear from you so soon. Why are you calling from the road?"

"I was just wondering. Do any of the kids at your church have the chickenpox?"

"Yeah. About a half dozen of them do. How did you know?"

"Oh. You know how some folks channel ancient warriors? I'm channeling childhood diseases."

"You've got the chicken pox? Now *that's* funny."

I hung up on him.

I pictured all the kind folks who had taken me in from Edmonton to Thunder Bay. "Typhoid Mary" now had a cycling compatriot—"Chickenpox Willie."

Once I got the go ahead from the hospital, I purchased a one-way plane ticket, boxed up my bike, and flew to Elmira, New York (where the family reunion was to be held).

I cannot begin to summon up words to describe the intensity of itching that comes from the combination of the chicken pox and six million black fly bites. My Uncle Joe actually used a paint roller to apply calamine lotion to my entire body. I looked like a leprosy victim who had been dipped in Pepto-Bismol.

Night after endless night I lay motionless in bed and with every ounce of my being I fought the urge to scratch. To give into this primal need would secure me a new nickname. Scarface. There is nothing quite as exhausting as not doing something.

Miraculously, about a week and a half later, I was feeling better. The scabs were dropping off like so much dandruff and Uncle Joe retired the paint roller. I could fly back and continue my trip, if only I had money. I was completely broke.

My big brother Jeff came to the rescue. Before I could even muster up the words to ask him he said over the phone, "Here's my VISA card number and the expiration date, get yourself a plane ticket back to Thunder Bay. You've got the rest of Canada to pedal across."

Almost two weeks after I had pedaled into Thunder Bay to the hospital, I once again pedaled from the airport into the city limits.

But I was not in high spirits.

I still itched. I'd lost a half a month of travel time to a comedic virus and I was pedaling into a stiff head wind.

"This sucks! Life sucks! Bicycles, black flies and ..."

My rant was cut short by the fixed gaze of a man whose face and body I instantly knew, but whom I'd never had the honor to meet.

It was Terry Fox. I stared up at the bronze statue of the Canadian hero who had lost a leg to cancer and had set out to run across Canada to raise money and awareness for cancer research. He began in Newfoundland on April 12, 1980, averaging nearly forty kilometers each day. He collapsed in Thunder Bay on September 1. That's as far as he got. He died a few months later.

It was one of those moments that instantly puts head winds, chickenpox, black flies and life into perspective. I pedaled out of Thunder Bay toward Nova Scotia, a humbled and forever thankful traveler.

THE DRINKING FOOL

In the hot Guatemalan sun I couldn't get enough of it. But the water I was drinking was far from refreshing. I was on a budget and couldn't afford a water filter, so I carried a bottle of iodine crystals. Each sip from my water bottle was tepid with a nauseatingly iodine aftertaste. Over the years of cycle touring, I had managed to get used to the cramped tent, the sore butt ... but never the lukewarm water.

It was a small price to pay, though, to cycle through a country with ancient Mayan ruins, papayas the size of watermelons, and trees that exploded with parrots or squealing monkeys as you pedaled by.

In midday the weather approximated an oven set on "Broil". I stopped at each body of water no matter how small, to soak my T-shirt and wash the stinging sweat from my eyes. As I cycled through a river valley sprinkled with cacti, I noticed a sign tacked up on a tree next to a shack on the side of the road. It read *Agua de Caña* (sugar cane juice). I had never tried this sweet treat and now seemed the perfect time.

The two boys working the stand gathered long stalks of sugar cane and fed them through the wheels of a metal extractor. The liquid half filled a small glass. While one boy accepted my *quetzal* as payment (twenty cents) the other boy took a cup full of water from a bowl on the floor that had the tiny remains of ice cubes in it and added it to my drink.

Warning lights flashed in my brain. "Don't drink it you fool. That water hasn't been boiled or treated in any way. This is how people get dysentery." I hesitated, but the thought of drinking one more gulp of iodine made me want to wretch. I drank the cool liquid and then held the glass against my forehead.

Back on the bike the flat river terrain turned to hilly as I turned toward Guatemala City.

It wasn't until the next morning that I felt the effects of my glass of *agua de caña*. At first I thought it was the heat as I struggled to climb up a moderate grade. But soon I found myself pushing my right leg down with my hand to complete a stroke. Later I got off my bike and pushed. Finally I sat down in the ditch on the side of the road. My head spun and my stomach did acrobatics.

A military van with thick, bullet-proof windows pulled off the road. A man jumped out and asked me in Spanish if I wanted a ride to Guatemala City. They were from the Guatemalan consulate, and had just taken a top U.S. military official on a sightseeing excursion to the ancient ruins of Tikal. The general had flown back in a helicopter so there was room in the van.

Never in my bicycle touring career had I accepted a ride. But I also had never felt so sick. I swallowed my pride (which was the only thing I could swallow at the time) and climbed into the vehicle.

The next forty-five minutes were the longest of my adult life. While the van sped along steep, bumpy, winding roads I leaned on my bike and tried to force my brain to focus on anything but the inevitable—I was about to vomit all over the Guatemalan consulate's brand new bullet proof van.

As the kilometers clicked away I thought of my high school girlfriends, summer camp, I tried to mentally list all the elements on the periodic chart (I managed six)—all while my stomach crept up toward my Adam's apple. I knew if I opened my mouth to plead for the driver to stop the results would be a very messy international incident.

We hit the Guatemala City limits and the driver finally pulled over to let one of his compatriots out. I elbowed my way passed him, knelt down in the street and gave up all the contents of my gastro-intestinal tract.

My bicycle was handed down to me and with an embarrassed smile I indicated I'd be all right. The van sped off in a large cloud of diesel exhaust.

I was so weak now I could barely walk. I shuffled to the side of the road and stuck out my thumb. An hour later I managed to get a ride into Antigua.

This was the one place in Guatemala where I had a contact. The year before I had cycled from San Diego, CA to Antigua, Guatemala and rented a room from a family for five weeks.

I limped into their courtyard and Florinda, dressed in tradi-tional Mayan clothes, greeted me with a smile that nearly cured me. Her four kids hung about my legs and jumped up and down crying "Weelee, Weelee." The family had one bed free and for the next four days I rarely left it. I drank water and worked my way up to fruit and then beans and rice. Within the week I felt healthy again and was eager to continue my journey.

I had learned my lesson. As I pedaled across the border into El Salvador I swore that I would make sure every drop of water was potable. And if it was suspect, I would gladly endure the vile taste of iodine.

The county had changed, but the heat had not. I pulled up to a newly built gas station and leaned my bicycle against the building. The shop next door was selling ice-cold slushes. The owner assured me the water they used was purified and he tapped a large five-gallon container of bottled water.

I sat down next to my bike and crunched and slurped the pineapple flavored treat. But my head soon ached from the cold (a classic brain freeze) and I looked around for relief. There next to me was a five-gallon pure water jug like the one in the store. It even had a hand push pump. I pumped in a few strokes of warm water over my icy slush and brought the temperature down to a brain-tolerable level. I filled my cup a second time from the water container. This was heaven as only a traveler can understand.

As I filled my cup the third time the gas station attendant glanced up and a look of horror came over his face.

"No. No. *Muy peligro!*" he shouted as he came running over to me.

The container I had been drinking from did not hold purified water after all, but water for his customers to wash their windshields.

I walked over to my panniers, took out six Pepto-Bismol tablets and some antibiotics, swallowed them, and prayed.

STEREOTYPES

IF YOU AND your spouse were invited by four hunters into a cabin in the backwoods of Alabama, at least three miles from a paved road, would you think twice before accepting their invitation? If the wall adornments included an Alabama license plate with two bullet holes, a dusty calendar from 1989 and a .22-caliber rifle flanked by "No Hunting" signs, would you be a little nervous? If the food in the kitchen consisted off Slim Jims, Cheese Nips, boiled peanuts, pork rinds, Swisher Sweets cigars, three 12-packs of Coke, a couple of quart bottles of Jim Beam, and no less than six cases of beer, would you find yourself heading quickly out the door?

I think most people would. Of course, most people would never travel the backcountry roads of Alabama in the first place.

I have cycled in India, Albania, Bosnia and El Salvador and do you know what the most common comment was from friends and acquaintances when I told them Kat and I would be cycling the Deep South?

"Oh. So your most dangerous journey to date."

Why the widespread deep fear of the Deep South?

A friend of mine, Tom Gerald, who is from the South, and a fine Southern gentleman he is, said that there were two movies made that did more to destroy tourism in the Deep South than just about anything else—*Deliverance* and *Easy Rider*. I think he's right.

To refresh your memory, since it's been over three decades since these films debuted, in *Deliverance*, Ned Beattie is forced to squeal like a pig while being sexually assaulted by a couple of Southern backwoods hunters. In *Easy Rider*, Dennis Hopper and Peter Fonda are blown off their Harley Davidsons by a couple of stereotypical Southern yahoos with shot guns.

It is hard to erase these strong images out of one's mind ... as stereotypical as they may be.

Our bicycle journey throughout South Carolina, Georgia, Alabama, Mississippi and Louisiana was filled with images and people who fit much of my pre-conceived, broad-stroke depiction of the South. But there was always a twist.

There was Elizabeth: A cute little woman in her late seventies we met in Georgia. She's a former schoolteacher with a wide smile and a gravelly laugh who could really spin a yarn. I looked at her and thought, "bake sale, knitting circle, wouldn't and couldn't harm a fly." Do you know what she has for protection? A .357 Magnum ... with a laser site. To hear this sweet little lady calmly and frankly talk about "putting that little red dot where it needs to go and all your troubles are behind you" was absolutely surreal.

One night Kat and I slept on the floor of a single-wide trailer. Guests of a muscular, sinewy man in his fifties named Billy. (Never mind how we got there, it just happened.) Billy has wild eyes and the uninhibited body movements and postures of an eight year-old. He works for Freightliner as a mechanic. He drinks substantial amounts of gin and Coke. He has a rifle conveniently hanging over the inside front door of his trailer. Do you want to hazard a guess at what I promised to mail to Billy when we returned to Seattle? Dahlia tubers. You read that right. The man loves to garden.

Now if I had told you that Billy owned a Magnum with a laser site and Elizabeth couldn't wait to receive a special garden package from the Northwest ... then everything and everyone would fit the mold. Pure stereotypes are what you get on TV. But travel takes all the stereotypical elements and shakes them up ... and like a kaleidoscope the picture never comes out exactly the same.

Years ago, while cycling a back road of Romania, Kat and I came upon a family of Gypsies. They were traveling in a wooden wagon, slowly drawn by an old plow horse. Walking behind their wagon, attached by a thick metal chain, was a pathetic looking black bear. My only previous encounter with Gypsies was in the lyrics of a bad seventies hit by Cher. Many locals had reminded us that Gypsies were to be avoided. They were dirty. They were liars. They were, in fact, all thieves.

As we pedaled by, I glanced up at the old man holding the reigns. I figured he was probably the grandfather: An illiterate man who made his living by forcing a poor bear to perform silly tricks for tourists. I pitied him.

About a mile up the road, Kat and I pulled over for a bite to eat. We had a fresh loaf of bread and fresh honey a local farmer had given us. Ten minutes later, the Gypsy wagon finally caught up to us. They pulled off the road as well and the old man, tethered the horse to a tree and approached us.

My first thought was, "There goes the rest of our lunch. This man is going to offer to have his bear dance a jig in exchange for the remains of our bread and honey and a few American dollars." Maybe we could quickly hop on our bikes and make our escape.

But he was rather fleet of foot for an old man, and was standing next to us before I could pack away our food.

The words that came tumbling out of his mouth in perfect English shocked me. He did not ask us for money, or for food, or to sit and watch his bear perform tricks. He asked us where we were from. When we told him the United States, he asked us what we thought of the candidates for the upcoming presidential primaries and then proceeded to list no less than eight of the primary contenders.

I was so busy feeling ashamed for having jumped like a trained circus bear into a stereotypic conclusion about this man's life, that I can't remember my response to his questions.

I'd like to believe I learned my lesson once-and-for-all that afternoon in Romania. But it is a lesson that must be revisited time and again.

As Mark Twain so eloquently put it in *The Innocents Abroad*, "Travel is fatal to prejudice, bigotry, and narrow-mindedness."

Kat and I stayed with those four aforementioned hunters in Alabama. Four of the finest gentlemen we met on our trip. We all fished for bass, watched the sunset streak the sky red and purple and counted shooting stars late into the night ... while eating Slim Jims and sipping beer.

THE ROLLER COASTER

I RODE THE roller coaster in Georgia. No, not the amusement park variety, and I'm not referring to the terrain—the roads Kat and I pedaled, through tree farms and cotton country, were mostly flat.

On a sparsely trafficked, sunny Sunday morning we pedaled from South Carolina to Georgia over a dramatic arching bridge and arrived in old historic Savannah. We strolled through the old live oak covered squares. We found a great coffee shop and a wonderful art gallery. This was my introduction Georgia. I loved it. I wanted to move there. It was winter and I was strolling through an art gallery in my shorts.

The next day we cycled out of Savannah and within five miles we were in strip mall suburbia hell. The six lanes bulged with traffic. Everyone was in a hurry and too many vehicles were coming way too close to our tandem bicycle. Then someone yelled and threw a fast-food bag of garbage at us. It glanced off of Kat's back. My opinion of Georgia dove as fast as the NASDAQ on a bad day. I hated Georgia. It was crowded and noisy and dangerous. I obsessed on the litter strewn along the side of the highway all of which, I was convinced, had been thrown at cyclists.

My mood sank even lower when twenty miles later we pulled into a campground. The man wanted to charge us twenty-eight dollars to pitch our tent. I was ready to turn around and head back to South Carolina. Maybe just catch a flight back to Seattle.

We pedaled on and asked a man in a Chevy pick-up if we could camp on his property.

"Sure can. I got 250 acres. Camp anywhere you'd like."

The spiral downward leveled off. Then the man in the truck turned around.

"Follow me. I'll show you a good place to camp out by our pond."

We followed him down a pine tree lined road and I was no longer heading back to South Carolina.

"Forget about settin' up your tent and sleep in our trailer," he said. "And if you want to build a fire, there's a pit and there's plenty of wood stacked up over there."

My opinion of Georgia had fully rebounded.

But the following day I talked with a man who owned a small store. We looked out at a huge pile of gravel that has just been delivered and I asked him if he was going to spread it out on his parking area.

"Nah. I'll get my nigga to do that."

Georgia took a long steep dive. Why did I want to waste my time traveling in this crowded, littered state filled with racist rednecks?

And on and on and on the roller coaster went—dipping and climbing—sometimes thrilling and sometimes nauseating.

This experience is not unique to Georgia. Combine the anxious anticipation of months (if not years) of dreaming and planning for a journey with the raw emotion that comes with actually beginning it, and you have a volatile mix. This is why I call the first week of a journey "riding the roller coaster."

When you begin a journey, as hard as you may try to avoid doing so, you take the first few days' experiences and extrapolate into the future.

Ride in a downpour the first day out ... you'll imagine Noah's Ark-like rain for the next eight weeks. Headwinds the first two days ... you'll swear that global warming has affected the earth's atmosphere, forcing the air currents to permanently travel in a westerly direction. Find yourself fixing three flats on the first day ... you'll convince yourself by the end of your journey you'll earn a place in the Guinness Book of World Records. "A touring cyclist managed to have 4,249 flats on a modest journey across the United States. The trip (originally planned to take three months) lasted two and a half years. The astonishing rate of one flat every 1.0087 miles is unprecedented in modern travel."

Get ready to ride the roller coaster multiple times in an extended journey. Borders (even borders between states) start the ride all over again. You may have just enjoyed four magical weeks in Germany, but if on your first day of cycling in France, you are chased by a wild pack of standard poodles, you'll be back at the emotional amusement park.

The key to surviving this emotional ride is acknowledging you're on one to begin with. It also helps to understand that the ride smoothes out over time. Why is that?

Maybe the best way to explain it is through our national pastime ... baseball. In the first week of a new season a batter's average (let's call him George) jumps all over the place. George goes four-for-four on opening day and he's batting a thousand. Perfect. Then he has the misfortune to face Roger Clemens the next day and goes zero-for-four. George is now batting .500. A 500-point drop in one day. But take that same lousy performance on the last day of a 162-day season, and George's average will drop a point, two maybe.

Three weeks into our Georgia journey if someone had thrown a beer can at us, our overall opinion of the state would have been barely affected. Rather than sending us into an emotional tailspin, it would have been absorbed into the thousands of experiences we'd had. Beyond the roller coaster is a smoother perspective—a more accurate average.

As much as I have traveled, I have never been able to avoid the raging peaks and valleys of emotion and opinion that come with the beginning of a journey. If it were all smooth sailing (or pedaling) we wouldn't call them adventures, would we?

I was afraid of roller coasters when I was a kid. I was convinced no matter how tightly I was strapped in, at the first extreme corner I would be flung off to my certain death. As an adult and as a traveler, I've learned to breath deep, relax … and enjoy the ride.

WORLDS APART

WAY OFF THE beaten path in Alabama not far from the Mississippi state line a teenage boy uttered the following:

"Daddy. You ain't gonna believe this. There's a man in bicycle britches at the door looking for a place to camp."

Daddy suggested the old ball field over the rise before shutting the door.

That might have been the end of the exchange right there. But Daddy's wife thought those travelers might be cold in the rain. They packed up some homemade deer stew and some sweet tea in the pickup truck and went searching for them.

They didn't find us at the ball field. Enough rain had fallen that it more closely resembled the Okeefenoke swamp. We quickly decided it was too wet to camp and pedaled up the road to try and locate a flat piece of higher ground. The sun was setting fast, we were soaked to the bone and the temperature was dipping into that hypothermia range. Just when life couldn't get more miserable, the harsh hissing of a rear-tire flat announced that "Yes, it could." By the time Daddy found us, we had all our gear strewn about on the side of the road.

Todd Skinner (his friends call him "Skin") and his wife Kim picked us up (along with our tandem bike) and brought us home.

"I would have picked up a stray dog in that kind of weather," Todd would later admit.

Kim showed Kat to the shower while Todd led me out to where we could sleep—his large garage/workshop. He stoked a metal barrel-shaped stove to take the chill off, while I cleared a space for our air mattresses and sleeping bags not far from the stove and near a muddy, knobby-tired ATV.

This might not sound like the best of accommodations, but when the alternative is pitching a tent in a bog with a relentlessly cold drizzle falling, a dry patch of concrete looks just fine.

Before dinner we were treated to some turkey calling. Todd's son and a friend were going to be off at the break of day to hunt wild turkey. As big as they are, they are apparently incredibly difficult to hunt. Your best bet is to hide in the woods and call them. They demonstrated various apparatus to mimic an authentic turkey call, from a piece of specially formed plastic you hold in your mouth, to a special piece of wood that you scrape with an equally special piece of wood to talk turkey.

I sat there thinking, "Why would anyone spend that kind of money to sound like a turkey whilst shivering in camouflage in the dawn's early light?"

Of course, I'm sure that Todd's son looked at me and wondered why anyone would spend that kind of money on a vehicle that you had to pedal and was so slow you had to rise before dawn to get anywhere?

After Kat and I had both showered, we spent the evening as guests at their table, eating the best stew east or west of the Mississippi and drinking enormous glasses of sweet tea.

Todd was raised not far down the road by a daddy who quit work every year come hunting season. He's taken up his daddy's passion, hunting and running deer with his eleven Walker hounds. He's a granddaddy at thirty-seven years old and works with his wife Kim at the paper mill thirty miles away. His sister is as mean as a snake, but would do anything for you if she liked you. His world revolves around his family, his land and the woods. But he is most alive when he's out in those woods, stalking a deer with a bow or listening for his hounds.

I looked across the dinner table at Todd and thought, "We are as different as night and day." He lives in the country. I live in the city. He voted for George. I voted for Al. He hunts for deer. I hunt for bargains at the grocery store. He drives a four-ton pick-up. I pedal a twenty-five-pound bike.

In our everyday lives, we'd never meet. Yet there we were telling stories and laughing around the dinner table.

We had no way of planning our stay with Todd and Kim. All I know is that it never would have happened if we'd had a reservation at a campground or a B&B. Sometimes having no plan is the best plan.

Dinner broke up around 9 PM. Kat and I headed out to the garage to hit the sack and Todd and Kim climbed in their truck to hit the road to arrive at the mill for the night shift. Jobs are scarce in small-town Alabama. Most folks drive sixty, a hundred, sometimes two hundred miles round trip to get to their jobs.

Before they left Todd said, "If it's raining like this tomorrow, no use in you going anywhere. I'll stock you up with plenty of wood and you feel free to stay another day."

We snuggled up in our sleeping bags close to the warm glow of the stove.

At 5 AM I opened my eyes as my dream-clogged brain tried to piece together where I was: rain pounding on a tin roof, the smell of hay and grease, the swaying silhouettes of Bradford pear trees through a workshop window, the yelp of a Walker hound. I was deep in the Deep South.

Todd and Kim arrived back home around 9 AM, invited us in for breakfast, and then went to bed—but not before Kim fixed us up with more coffee and sandwiches for lunch.

We spent the cold, drizzly day in our makeshift guesthouse reading, writing letters and relishing the simple pleasure of being cozy and warm and dry. Our routine established, we came in later for another home-cooked supper and swapped stories until Todd and Kim left for the mill.

The next morning brought partially cloudy skies but no rain. We'd packed up our bikes and were called in for breakfast. Todd and I walked out to the workshop after we'd all had our fill of pancakes. The air was crisp with a hint of pine and hay and our boots squished through the spring rain mud. He asked me to help him load some hay onto the truck for his cows. My legs were strong from many weeks of pedaling, but my arms were still those of a city boy. As I struggled with a bale I mentioned, "You know, Todd, I bet if I was born out here, I would have been a farmer *and* a hunter."

He smiled, whisking the bale out of my arms as if it weighed nothing, saying, "And if I'd been born in the city. I'd probably been a bike rider."

DEFINING ADVENTURE

Adventure. It is one of my favorite words in the English language. The mention of it congers up vivid images and experiences. It gets my heart pumping and my adrenaline rushing.

Sadly though, my favorite word is being used so often it is in danger of becoming a cliché.

The automobile industry promises adventure with every SUV they sell. Dating services promise adventure and lifelong love and the tourism industry uses adventure to charge more for a package deal.

So what is adventure?

The *American Heritage Dictionary* defines the noun "adventure" as:

1.a. An undertaking or enterprise of a hazardous nature. b. An undertaking of a questionable nature, especially one involving intervention in another state's affairs.

The *Webster's Revised Unabridged Dictionary* defines the verb "adventure" as:

1.To risk, or hazard; jeopard; to venture. 2. To venture upon; to run the risk of; to dare.

Not a single dictionary I checked defined adventure without using the words risk or hazard.

If I except dictionary definitions of adventure then the adventure travel industry is rarely about adventure. It is about the exotic. It is about extravagance. It is all about catered meals and scheduled events.

I worked as a bicycle tour guide for four years. I loved it. Loved the people. Loved the scenery. Loved the food (had the extra pounds to prove it). Loved the cycling. Was it an adventure? In my own opinion ... no.

My guests knew when they were going to get up, what they were going to have for breakfast, and how many miles to a catered picnic lunch. They knew that a cold beer would be waiting at the hotel or bed-and-breakfast, what pricey restaurant they'd be dining in that evening, and if I had spare time, that their luggage was waiting for them in their room with a view.

Most people want adventure without the risks, hazards and discomforts.

In other words, most people want adventure—without the adventure.

This type of travel in the tourism industry is often referred to as "soft adventure" or "adventure lite." Guests are paying premium dollars for their adventure to be scheduled, organized and safe.

I have heard more than one adventure travel guide joke that it is their job to make sure their guests don't have an adventure because if they do, more often than not, they want their money back. And if they have an extreme adventure, they'll sue.

How do you know when you're in the midst of an adventure?

Ask yourself these questions:

"Am I beyond my comfort zone?"

"Am I pushing my physical limits?"

"Am I taking a risk?"

If your answer is no to all of these answers, chances are you are not on an adventure. When was the last time you read a best-selling adventure travel narrative by someone who went on a guided or catered tour? If on every night of your travels you are drinking a cold beer, eating wonderful food and sleeping in a comfortable bed ... you're on vacation.

And that's okay. Sometimes a bike trip is simply just a wonderful bike trip.

By the way, *The American Heritage Dictionary* defines vacation as:

A period of time devoted to pleasure, rest, or relaxation, especially one with pay granted to an employee.

Adventure is hard to define and even harder to quantify. What's adventure for one individual is routine for another. You can't categorize adventure by the activity. Is cycling packed and unsupported an adventure? Is riding unburdened on an organized trip a vacation? Not necessarily.

Years ago I was leading a cushy trip through the San Juan Islands. I had just finished fitting my last rider to their rental bike, and I noticed one of my guests was trying to get my attention. She waited for everyone to leave and then approached me. She looked up at me and said, "How do you work this thing?"

I would have laughed, but I saw the fear in her eyes. She went on to explain that she hadn't been on a bike since she was five years old. She had signed up for this trip to force herself to leap over a fear.

I took her out to the parking lot of the bed-and-breakfast and taught her how to shift the gears and work the brakes. I thought she was going to pass out as she held onto the handlebars with a death grip as she timidly made her way around asphalt.

The next morning I passed her in the van as she pedaled to the ferry dock. Her smile and exuberance were that of a little kid.

Same trip. Different experiences. Her fellow guests were on vacation. She was on an adventure.

There are many people who will say, "Every time I ride my bike I'm on an adventure." Using the term adventure to describe every moment in the saddle cheapens it. See adventure as something not so easily attained—as something to strive for.

For many years, I have used facing a fear as my own personal yardstick for adventure. I don't limit this to physical fears of danger and travel, but to emotional fears, cultural fears and spiritual fears as well.

If I defined adventure as encompassing every moment I spent on the bike, I'd probably still not own a passport. I'd be perfectly contented to pedal within the boundaries of the United States.

My personal definition of adventure has pushed me to pedal into the homelands of South Africa when everyone around me told me I'd lose my life there as a white man. It has pushed my cultural limits in small villages in India. It has challenged me to see Bosnia while troop trucks and tanks were the norm. And it has prodded me to spend three months in Cuba even though my government said I couldn't.

I'm sure my answer to "what is adventure?" will change as I grow older and hopefully wiser and thus continue to challenge me.

Adventure by definition isn't easy … and personally, I wouldn't have it any other way.

BUSY SIGNAL

IN 1995, WHEN I left for a five-month bicycle journey through South Africa, I told friends and family that I would be writing a column for the *Global Network Navigator* on the World Wide Web. They all responded, "The World Wide What???" That was back when travel agents still roamed the earth and before Google was a verb.

I cannot think of anything that has changed travel more than the Internet: from researching a destination, to booking tickets, to corresponding while on the road.

Does anyone remember postcards? They had glossy, often silly photos on one side and another side that was blank and you were supposed to fill it with travel memories and banal sentiments. For close friends, your handwriting was microscopic, allowing you to pen the equivalent of the first chapter of Moby Dick, while you drastically enlarged it for acquaintances and workmates. These cards were physically "mailed" and often arrived two weeks after your return home.

Today you can cycle up to an Internet café and blast off a trip report to the 600 people on your email list before you are halfway through your double shot mocha. It has never been easier to stay in touch.

Here's a thought: how can you be missed if you are never out of touch?

Do you remember the days when you fantasized about what your friends were doing on a long bicycle journey, hoping for a letter in the mail? Now forget the letters and postcards. You get to read about their journeys in minute detail on a daily or even hourly basis. By the time they return home, all the romance is gone. You don't want to sit down and have a beer and be regaled with stories of the road. You've already heard them all.

"You can't be in two places at once," they used to say. Well, thanks to the Web, you can. You can travel in a foreign country and still live your life at home: paying bills online, answering emails, reading the daily newspaper, updating your website (don't forget your blog). The Internet can be the world's longest umbilical cord.

Most travelers will tell you that it takes a week or two on the road before you truly leave your workaday world behind and begin to fully immerse yourself in your travel—the sites, the smells, the language, and the culture of a new place.

But thanks to the Internet you can walk into a cyber café 8,000 miles away from home and, click, you're back.

Isn't it ironic that we can spend hundreds of hours in front of a computer screen researching and dreaming of traveling in a distant land, then the first thing we do when we arrive there is to seek out a computer screen, only to stare at news and photos of the place we've just left?

Before the age of the Internet, my contact with home consisted of a weekly or bimonthly three-to-five minute call. That was it, other than occasionally coughing up the dough to invest in the international edition of *Time* magazine. I always found it amazing to return from a five-month journey and realize how little I'd missed. At home, I'd spend at least an hour a day reading the newspaper or newsmagazines, yet I could return to a mountain of papers and magazines and junk mail and push them off into the recycling bin.

I cycled around India in 1994. There were no cyber cafés and I couldn't afford the international calling rates.

I'm a diehard Seattle Mariners fan, and it was impossible to get updates and scores. I accosted the few fellow Americans I met on the road for a Major League baseball fix. The local and national Indian newspapers were worthless. Their sports pages were filled with cricket scores.

Somewhere in the desert region of Rajasthan, I finally gave up trying to find out about my favorite baseball team and began to actually read the articles about cricket. They didn't make much sense to begin with, but after a couple of months I had a pretty good handle on the national sport of India. By the time I watched part of a test match with some locals in Bangalore, I was able to hold my own discussing strategy.

In contrast, when Kat and I cycled in Turkey in 2003, we had no idea how wired the country was. Internet access turned out to be as easy to find as lamb kabob. If a town had more than 200 residents, they had a cyber café.

This was wonderful … and horrible.

Partway through our journey, an earthquake somewhere in the bowels of the sea snapped the high-speed access line to Turkey. Downloads went from seconds to hours. But I was there to get my Internet fix and I was going to get it. I sat in front of a screen for twenty-five minutes waiting for the home page of our mail server to come up, another fifteen minutes to logon and another twenty to download the messages and box scores. All for what? To read that the Seattle Mariners had lost three in a row and that, low and behold, it had been raining in the Pacific Northwest.

I hate to think about what parts of Turkish life and culture I missed out on because of the numerous hours I spent trying to stay in touch. What a waste!

If you have decided to travel in France ... live in France, eat in France, be in France. Make that trip to the cyber café your last resort, not your first stop. It's hard to resist the urge to plug into the digital umbilical cord when it is available 24/7. But each time you check the website of your local newspaper or check your email, you force your mind to travel back to the worries and complexities of another life you don't have much control over. Every minute, every hour that you spend focused on "home" is an hour not spent in France, or Africa or the back roads of Kentucky. And believe me, your mind will wander back home plenty often without the aid of the Web.

Am I advocating Internet abstinence? No.

Sure, you should continue to send email dispatches from the road. Sure, you should check in with friends and loved ones and let them know you are alive and well.

But how often is too often? Once a week? Once a day? On the hour, every hour? Continually? (Yes, continuous contact with home will be possible once cheap cell phone service goes global).

The answer is different for each of us, but, just as it is the key to riding a bicycle, it's all about finding and maintaining your balance.

GUARDIAN ANGELS

I HAD ALWAYS been a bicycle traveler—happy to see the world at a slower pace on a bicycle with fatter tires, racks and a kickstand. Not once had I been tempted to dawn skinny tires and race in a pack, no matter how many Tour de Frances I watched.

But there was another segment of the bicycle world that intrigued me. Its members were on the fringe. They got paid to ride their bikes and wear funky clothes. They were described as dangerous, free-spirited, counter-culture rebels.

I am speaking of the honored and sometimes vilified profession of bike courier.

Never would I have thought to interview for the job, accept that a friend said, "Willie, just think of it as ultra-light touring with dozens of destinations each day rather than one."

So on a whim I walked into the office of ENA couriers in Seattle and applied for a job. To my utter disbelief, I was hired immediately.

I was issued a canvas shoulder bag, a two-way radio and a red and gray Burley rain jacket. My first day on the job was tailing Robert, a young, black sinewy man who after eight hours of delivering packages, went to a martial arts gym and worked out for three hours.

The hundreds of mountains passes I'd climbed had done nothing to prepare me for a day with Robert. It took every once of stamina
I had just to keep him within sight.

Seattle is built on seven hills, and I'd swear we went up each of
them a hundred times before lunch. On one of our few breaks, we sat
in a city park. I was on my fourth peanut butter and jelly sandwich
and Robert was on his second set of fifty push-ups.

"Yeah. But the real question is, are you flexible," I quipped.

Robert stood up, gave me a wide grin and dropped into the
splits. That was it. I knew right then and there that he was either an
alien or a borg.

After what Robert told me was a typical eight hour day, I arrived
home a broken man. I ate a cold can of soup and collapsed into bed.
That first week was hell, but by the end of the second I had found
some new sprinting muscles and settled into a routine.

My number was "two-five" which was soon replaced with "Wild
Willie." My fellow couriers nicknamed me "Grandpa", because at
twenty-eight years old, I was the eldest by five years.

During my nine-month tenure I never had an accident, never
got a ticket and only hit one pedestrian (I glanced off the upheld
briefcase of a lawyer after my front brake cable broke coming down
Madison street). Overall, my career was pretty tame and would not
fill the annals of bike messenger legend ... except for one incident.

I had just finished delivering the last package in my bag at 12th
and Jackson. Jackson Street runs in a long downhill towards Seattle's
Pioneer Square and ENA's satellite bike office. I was coasting, enjoying a rare unrushed moment, soaking up some sun, which in itself
was rare for Seattle in March. At that moment I had the perfect job.

Two seconds later, the mood changed. The driver's side door of a brand new Porsche opened quickly and without warning three feet in front of me. My reactions took over. I swerved to the left to avoid being "doored" (as it's called in the business) and simultaneously checked traffic. I missed the leather-paneled door by inches and a Metro bus by a foot.

If it had been my first day of work, I'd have been sprawled out in the middle of Jackson Street. But six months into the job, the maneuver was as natural as reaching for a water bottle. It was routine. No big deal.

I stopped at a red light about two blocks further down the hill. The light turned green and as I reached the comfortable cruising speed of about seven miles per hour the Porsche pulled up alongside of me. The passenger, dressed in a silk business suit, had his window rolled down so I called out, "You need to look before opening your door."

I didn't expect an apology. In fact, I was ready to be the recipient of a couple of middle fingers and a snide remark. But what happened next took me by surprise. The driver got an incredulous look on his face and his buddy said, "Hey. I'll open *my* door anytime I'd like, you %!@#. In fact, I think I'll open it right now. With his final syllable, he swung his door open. I swerved and just barely missed a parked Subaru wagon.

In disbelief I stared at the man whose face was wracked with fury. Now the driver yelled out. "Get away from my car, you $#%$." We were pulling up to another red light. "Streets are for cars, you idiot. Get on the sidewalk. Go on. Am I going to have to get out and kick your @##?"

We now had come to a complete stop.

My reactions had been lightening fast to avoid the inanimate object, but now that I needed to avoid a physical confrontation, I froze up. I was a deer in the headlights, my mouth wide open in shock and amazement. I could have easily pedaled away, but all I could muster was the thought, "I am, in just a few seconds, going to get the crap beaten out of me. What an odd way to ruin a sunny day in Seattle."

The man advanced around the hood of his car and his friend was rising up from his fully adjustable bucket seat.

Suddenly, there was a horrendously loud screech as warn brake pads ground on warn brake drums. Both doors of a white Ford van simultaneously opened.

My Porsche buddies had friends and now I am going to die.

Two very large men emerged in white overalls covered with splotches of paint. One of them yelled over my shoulder to the businessmen. "We saw what happened back there and it was all your fault. So if you are going to fight this bicycle dude, you are going to have to fight us, too."

The two businessmen, leery of losing face on a public street, made a few derogatory comments under their breath, but seeing they had met their match, retreated to the safety of their vehicle.

"That's right," called one of the workers. "Get back in your #$%^&*! fancy car and go have a #$%^&*! three martini lunch, you #$%^."

The Porsche screamed off toward Pioneer Square. The taller of the two workers gave me a smile, the other a thumbs up. They jumped in their van, made a quick U-turn and headed east back up the hill.

Me? I stood there through another cycle of the traffic light, pondering what my fate would have been without divine intervention.

I had always heard stories about guardian angels. How they magically appeared in all manner of manifestations. I'd always been a skeptic. They were the subjects of silly tales in magazines and television series. But I am alive today to give witness that I have met my heavenly guardians. They are cleverly disguised as tough-talking painting contractors and drive a white Ford van.

FEAR FACTOR

TERRORIST ATTACKS. NINE-ELEVEN. War in Iraq. Osama bin-Laden. Al-Qaida. Reprisals against Americans. Weapons of mass destruction.

Newspapers, television, radio and the Web are filled with terror and fear.

What is a traveler to do during the "War on Terror?"

We could all stay home. Cancel our long-planned journeys. Put them on hold until it's over. But how long will that be? And who is going to declare that it's over?

I live by a couplet that helps me keep it all in perspective:

"Caution keeps you aware. Fear keeps you away."

Caution is active. It seeks to solve problems, to move forward. Caution helps you make the kinds of decisions that keep you safe: to wear reflective clothing, to check your shoes for scorpions, to heed storm warnings, to avoid large groups of drunken sports fans.

Fear is passive. It lies in the pit of your stomach and festers. Fear doesn't do anything but freeze you in life's headlights. It stomps out dreams and makes you old before your time.

Everywhere and every time I've decided to travel, there has always been a host of people telling me that I should be afraid. In Mexico I was supposed to be afraid of the drug traffickers and the bad drivers; in Central America it was the drug traffickers and the guerillas. In India it was the diseases; in South Africa it was the black-on-white violence; in Bosnia it was the landmines.

Even in a country as benignly safe as Canada I was warned. In the middle of Ontario, I met a couple of cyclists from British Columbia who were cycling across their country. They asked me if I was going to cycle into Quebec.

When I responded, "Of course," they asked me if I spoke French.

I told them I didn't speak a word.

For the next forty-five minutes they told me how badly I would be treated there and advised me to avoid the province altogether. Turns out, that was exactly their plan. These two Canadians whose dream it was to cycle across their country, were dipping into New York, Vermont and New Hampshire in order to bypass the province of Quebec.

They told me of English speaking travelers being refused service in restaurants, thrown out of bars, spat on, and run off the road.

When I prodded them for their sources, they could never quite remember. Every story was from a friend of a neighbor or a sister's boyfriend's uncle. But these stories had put enough fear in them to change the course of their journey.

We parted ways and I cycled east toward the evil empire of Quebec, where I was to never once take my tent out of my panniers. Every single night I was invited into someone's home.

These two lads had forgotten to use "the fear filter." It is a very simple and effective tool that will allow your travel horizons to expand to the furthest reaches of the globe. I have used it effectively for over twenty years now. It is a phrase that consists of four simple words: *Have—you—been—there?*

Here's how it works. Whenever someone begins to tell you about the dangers and horrors of the country where you've planned a trip ... use the fear filter ... "Have you been there?" Cut them off mid-sentence with this question. I guarantee you that nine times out of ten their answer will be "no". And when it is, simply put up your hand and say, "Sorry, I don't want to hear it."

You will be amazed at how positive the opinions of a country or region will be when you only solicit views from people who have lived or traveled there.

Another fear factor that crops up now more than ever is the anxiety of anti-American feelings throughout the globe. People are canceling trips not only to the Middle East, but to France and Germany as well. Sure it might be safe to travel there, but once you admit that you are an American, the party's over. You'll be run out of town on a rail.

Many who decide to go, plan to don maple leaf flags on their panniers and become Canadians for the duration of their tour.

I have always admitted my United States citizenship when asked, everywhere I've traveled—even in Serb-controlled Bosnia in 1996 with troops and tanks on the highways. Not once have I had someone treat me unkindly because I admitted to being an American.

It helps that I am seen as a traveler first, someone who is interested enough in the country he's traveling in to take the time and effort to cycle through it. But the fact is that most people around the world do not want to be judged by the actions and policies of their government. In many countries around the world, people have little or no say in what their government does. What people think and what their government thinks are two completely different entities.

Now if you decide to cycle into Paris, wearing a T-shirt that boldly states, "I only eat Freedom Fries," all bets are off. You're on your own.

Kat and I are currently packing for our next adventure: Turkey. The U.S. military has just bombed Iraq in a campaign called "shock and awe." No, we didn't choose our destination because of the present situation in the Middle East. We decided on a three-month journey in Turkey over a year and a half before the invasion.

We have been using "the fear filter" often this last couple of weeks. We have been warned not to go by friends, neighbors, our mail carrier, the guy who walks his yappy dogs by our house and countless others. They all have one thing in common. Yep. They have never been to Turkey.

There has not been a single person to date who has traveled in Turkey who has warned us not to go. On the contrary, they tell us how the already low prices will be lower; how the locals will be grateful we are helping the struggling tourist economy.

We are going because the alternative is to be imprisoned by our fears, to remain under house arrest until the media declares that we are free to travel.

The world needs ambassadors of peace and goodwill now more than ever. I can't think of a better vehicle for the job than a loaded down bicycle. So plan a journey, listen to only those who have gone before you, be cautious, and have the adventure of a lifetime.

THE BAD ROAD

STRADDLING OUR FULLY loaded mountain bikes at an intersection during peak rush hour we were faced with a decision—to take the small road over the mountains, or the main road around them.

This is usually a no-brainer. Take the small road, of course. But there were complicating factors. This intersection was in the city of Inegöl in western Turkey, and the four men surrounding our bikes were as adept at the English language as Kat and I were at Turkish. Two and a half days into a three-month journey, my Turkish vocabulary consisted of about twenty words, seventeen having to do with food.

We pointed to our map and outlined the main road through Domaniç.

"Good. Good. Yes." came the jumble of replies screamed over the din of traffic.

I then traced our preferred route, a thin gray line up into the mountains through a village named Boğazova.

They all shook their heads in unanimous disapproval and one man yelled, "No. Bad. Bad. Bad."

I turned to Kat, "This isn't just a bad road—it's a triple-bad road."

That should have sealed our decision right there. But the thought of taking the main road (which was sure to carry the bus and truck traffic) kept us frozen at the intersection.

What did the men mean that the road was "bad"? Did it travel through a region filled with packs of ravenous wolves? Was it paved with gravel the size of your fist? Was the map wrong and did the road dead-end up there somewhere above 6,000 feet?

Kat shouted as a bus filled with screaming students passed, "We can always turn around and take the main road if it doesn't work out."

Problem solved.

We pedaled off toward the mountain road while four Turkish men shouted and frantically waved for us to go in the opposite direction.

The mad combination of scooters, mini-busses, trucks and school kids on foot darting all about reminded me of India. We pedaled for our lives. Then as if some wizard had waved his magic wand ... we were out in the country. Most cities in Turkey lack suburbs, so the transition from urban to rural is as instantaneous as flipping a light switch. We were looking up at a row of eight-story apartment buildings and on the other side was a pastoral field with shepherds attending a herd of goats and sheep.

Evening was fast approaching, so we pitched our tent off the side of the road in a grove of cherry trees planted next to a rushing spring stream. *This* was a bad road?

We awoke to a brisk, crystal-clear morning. A quarter moon shown behind cherry blossoms. We packed up our tent, loaded the bikes and began climbing up into the mountains along a narrow, lazily winding paved road ... with not a motorized vehicle in sight.

There are moments in a bicycle journey (when the light is perfect, the weather sublime, the scenery a bag of eye candy) when I get downright giddy. A smile and a giggle emerge from my soul that melts away the years and I am seven years old again, without a care or worry in the world.

After about ten kilometers, we pedaled through a small village. The pavement gave way to a firm dirt road and the grade increased as we climbed higher into the mountains.

My own pre-conceived impression of Turkey as a dry, hot, dusty country, kept me from ever imagining (even though it was April) that we might hit snow if we pedaled up into the mountains.

By the time we reached the outskirts of the next village the temperature had plummeted and we were surrounded by pine trees, not cherry trees and our packed dirt road was getting soft. With the help of our pocket dictionary, we managed to ask a man walking along the road about the conditions further up. He looked at our vehicles of choice and shook his head. "Çok kar. Çok çamur." (Lot's of snow. Lot's of mud.)

In a very un-adventure cyclist reaction, I suggested we coast back down the mountain and try the other road. Kat took me aside and suggested we ask this man if there was somewhere we could stay in town and see what the next day would bring.

He was absolutely delighted that we wanted to stay in Boğazova and led us to his home. We removed our shoes outside the front door and across the small courtyard from the outhouse and stepped into a toasty-warm sitting room. His wife gave us an equally toasty-warm greeting and then opened up the oven and pulled out the largest loaf of bread we'd ever laid eyes on.

This large, thick circular loaf was just the beginning of an evening of Turkish delights. We soon learned that our host couple was childless (a rarity in Turkey) and they both loved to cook. As their surrogate kids for the evening, we were presented with a feast: Fresh, stream trout baked in their wood stove oven with cheese and slabs of butter; pilaf *and* potatoes; freshly made lentil soup; cooked tender nettles, a yogurt drink called *ayran* made from fresh yogurt and spring water; and to top off the right-out-of-the-oven bread, homemade sun-dried tomato paste with olive oil, walnuts and garlic.

After several post-dinner glasses of chai we were ushered into their bedroom and allowed to slip into deep food-induced comas.

In the morning, refreshed and rejuvenated, we decided to press on. Our hosts insisted on leading us out to the road. We wondered why they donned rubber boots until we turned a corner and spied a river of thick brown mud that *was* the main road. We laughed. This road was so atrocious it was comical. It wasn't triple-bad … it was five-star bad. But we'd made it this far … why not?

We waved good-bye to our hosts and began to slowly push our bikes through the brown ooze. We managed about two kilometers over the next hour and then it began to rain. A cold drizzle just this side of snow had us both wondering why we decided to leave our warm guesthouse in Boğazova. Then it dawned on us that as well as we'd been fed, we'd managed to leave town without stocking up on any provisions.

As we climbed higher into the mountains, the temperature steadily dropped. The mud thickened, allowing us to occasionally pedal. Just as hunger and hypothermia were creeping into our cores, we stumbled into a village. Our delight quickly dissipated as we stared at the closed sign on the only store.

A slight man, dressed in a wool cap and suit coat walked up to us and Kat asked where we might find bread. A smile spread across his face and within five minutes we were once again in the warm glow of a wood burning fire.

We were made to understand that we were honored guests. Our clothes would be washed and dried. We would be staying for lunch, then dinner and of course, we would be staying the night and Kat would receive a gift of hand knitted-slippers. We were learning first hand how few cultures on this planet could rival the hospitality of the Turks. After dinner the room filled up with sons, daughters, neighbors, friends, the schoolteacher and his wife—over twenty people in a ten-by-twelve foot room, drinking chai and snacking on popcorn and sunflower seeds. I glanced over at Kat on the other side of the room and we exchanged "can you believe we're here" smiles.

Who knows what kind of experiences would have befallen us on the main road. But I do know from a lifetime of experiences ... that the bad roads most often lead to the best adventures.

MT. NEMRUT

In southeastern Turkey, beyond Mt. Argeus and the major cities of Adiyaman and Malatya, is the archeological wonder of Mt. Nemrut. King Antiochus, a megalomaniac ruler in around 50 BC, decided to leave a lasting monument of his greatness. A nearby mountain wasn't impressive enough, so he ordered a 150-foot artificial peak of piled crushed rock to be erected. Two large ledges were cut out of the mountainside and filled with colossal statues of King Antiochus and the gods.

I stood marveling at this World Heritage site, which was only rediscovered in 1881, with its stunning views in every direction. My body tingled with goose bumps. Out there to the south was Syria. I was overwhelmed with vastness of space and the breadth of human history that had passed below me.

At my side was an Israeli tourist, a man in his sixties. We stood in silence, gazing at one of the enormous stone heads. After a while he leaned over and said, "It's not such a big deal, is it?"

Not such a big deal! Was he out of his mind?

How could two people stare up at the same archeological wonder and have such incredibly different reactions? Then it dawned on me. He hadn't taken the "bad" road.

He had approached Nemrut from the south aboard a fifty-passenger Mercedes tour bus. This luxury bus, with its padded seats and foot rests, came with an attendant who offered snacks and bottled water and warm face towels. The bus had wound its way up the mountain from the city of Adiyaman and parked not more than 500 meters from the summit.

We had cycled the alternate route, "the road less traveled." Mark Jenkins of *Outside* magazine calls it "the hard way." I use the term, "the bad road."

This was the route the busses avoided. Car rental agencies made you sign on the dotted line that you wouldn't even think driving on it. A route where the winds blew so hard at times you couldn't fall over if you tried.

The man behind the tourist information counter in Malatya had laughed when I asked about cycling to Mount Nemrut.

"You can try. No one will stop you," he said. "But you'll turn back. It's too difficult."

What self-respecting adventure cyclist could turn down a challenge like that?

Kat and I agreed we'd give it our best. We cycled out of the city of Malatya in the early morning to beat the rush-hour traffic. The traffic disappeared the moment we turned off the main highway and we soon found ourselves high up into the foothills. Apricot trees in large groves as far as the eye could see. Malatya is considered the apricot capital of the world for good reason.

The road wound up into the mountains, passed tiny villages, each with a prominent minaret atop the local mosque. The afternoon call to prayer echoed up from the valley. For over fifteen miles the road ascended. We were alone except for occasional sightings of sheep, goats, cattle and their attendants. The temperature dropped and the winds whipped up, forcing us to dig into our panniers for extra layers of clothing.

Several hours later at the top of the climb, we were greeted not by a plateau, but by a steep downhill grade. We descended mile after mile. Don't get me wrong. I love down hills. But when your final destination is a mountaintop a seemingly endless descent gets rather depressing at a certain point.

After steeply descending several thousand feet, we stopped to rest our hands from the stress of gripping our brakes. A group of primary school teachers spotted us. Minutes later, we found ourselves in a classroom filled with Kurdish children dressed in their blue-and-white school uniforms.

We answered their questions with their teacher acting as interpreter. A classroom globe was brought out and we traced our route through Turkey and pinpointed our home in Seattle.

The teacher then asked one of the little girls to sing for us. She filled that little schoolroom with a hauntingly beautiful Kurdish folksong. The entire class joined her for the chorus.

We walked our bikes back to the road and continued our descent. A thunderstorm appeared out of nowhere and we pulled off the road and huddled beneath our ground tarp, shivering as sheets of rain poured over us.

Near dark we coasted, hungry and damp, into the village of Tepehan where another batch of teachers adopted us for the evening. Our bikes were stored in one teacher's room, while Kat and I stayed in the headmaster's apartment.

We awoke to a brilliantly crisp, blue-skied morning. Rested and well fed, we began the final ascent. We climbed for over eight hours.

The pavement had long since disappeared and the loose gravel was often so thick that pedaling was impossible. So we pushed and pedaled—and pushed some more.

On one of the several switch-backs, Kat, who is not a columnist for *Adventure Cyclist* magazine—who has not longed to cycle the world since she was sixteen—lay prostrate in the middle of the road and took my name in vain—several times.

But thanks to a bag of dried apricots from Malatya buried deep in a rear pannier, and the encouragement of local shepherd kids, we pushed on.

And after several hundred kilometers of sweat, tears and adventure, we arrived at the top of Mount Nemrut at exactly the same moment as an Israeli tourist who walked up from the parking lot on the other side.

No wonder our reactions were so different.

After five minutes, the disappointed tourist descended. Kat and I on the other hand, stayed and danced with Kurdish students who were visiting from their university. We danced at the foot of the statues of Nemrut, to the beat of drums and the melody of the *sorna*, a wind instrument related to the oboe.

But as the sun set, they too had to descend down to their tour busses, leaving Kat and I to camp at the edge of the mountain. We had Nemrut to ourselves, sharing it only with the one security guard and a young intrepid traveler from Siberia who had walked up our very same route.

Adventure is rarely determined by the destination you choose, but by the method of travel and route you take to get there.

Is it worth using your limited time to see all the archeological or tourist sites simply to check them off a list? Or is it better to see a handful of wonders that send shivers up your spine?

The bad road. The road less traveled. The hard way. Call it what you will, but be forewarned. Once you've tried it, you may discover that it's the only way.

FORGOTTEN TURKEY

A LARGE MILITARY vehicle sped by, kicking up rocks and a huge cloud of dust. I could make out through the brown haze a helmeted man behind a large machine gun mounted on a turret. The brakes squealed and it swerved to a stop about fifty feet in front of our bikes.

All four doors simultaneously opened and four soldiers with assault rifles jumped out and surrounded us.

As the dust cleared, a man wearing a military cap stepped out of the vehicle and approached us with his arms out and a smile on his face.

"Don't worry. Don't worry. We are here to protect you!"

Funny. I hadn't felt the need for protection prior to our sunny day's ride being so dramatically interrupted.

"You can travel anywhere in Turkey that you'd like," he continued in perfect English. But *this* road that you are on … you must have special permission."

"Also. You seemed to have passed a checkpoint back there. My friends waved at you, but you did not stop. You must have not heard their calls because of the wind."

His explanation was interrupted by an identically imposing military vehicle—with matching machine gun and turret—skidding to a halt behind us. Four more soldiers with assault rifles jumped out.

"If you trust us. We will put your bicycles in that vehicle and you will come with me in this vehicle and we will go back to the checkpoint and have a discussion."

As we roared down the highway, the soldier in the front passenger seat set down his assault rifle long enough to offer us a refreshing spritz of lemon cologne.

"Where did you learn your English?" I yelled over the din of the motor.

"I don't speak English," he smiled back.

"Where are you from?"

"I am from the heavens. I am your guardian angel." He winked. "I am also a PhD in information technology and human interaction."

Talk to most people who have visited Turkey and they will talk of the West: the grand mosques of Istanbul, the ruins of Ephesus, the aqua-blue waters of the Aegean Sea and the mystical and dramatic landscape of Cappadocia.

East of Cappadocia is the "other" Turkey. A region raw and far less traveled. This was evident as soon as we purchased maps for our journey. Western Turkey was shown in the scale of 1:800,000, while the Eastern Turkey only merited 1:2,000,000.

The Kurdish separatist movement in the nineties brought virtual civil war to the Southeast and over 30,000 people were killed in the fighting. The Kurds still refer to it as Kurdistan. The region is much more peaceful at present, but the military presence looms large.

Venturing into southeastern Turkey is not for cyclists who crave creature comforts. A comparison of roadside gas stations immediately lets you know where this region of Turkey lies on the tourist map.

In Western Turkey the gas stations remind me of the United States in the sixties. Smiling, uniformed attendants greet you, pump your gas, check your tires, wash your windows and offer you a cup of chai. If you are on a bicycle, they will more than likely invite you to sit down for a meal. The stations are spotless and have landscaping with trimmed shrubs and rose bushes. There are often picnic tables with umbrellas to shade you from the midday sun where you can enjoy your drinks and snacks purchased at the counter. The bathrooms are beautifully tiled and clean. In fact, there is no better place for a cyclist to stop and use the facilities than a petrol station in western Turkey.

In the East, more often than not, gas stations are dreary slabs of dusty concrete with pumps that may or may not work. An attendant might be roused if you knock loudly enough at the office door. If you are one who does not fancy relieving yourself outdoors, the toilets in these facilities just might make you change your mind.

The same comparison could be made for most amenities connected to tourism: roads, restaurants, hotels, and shops—they all are lacking in the East.

So why go? Why not avoid this region completely as do the other ninety-nine percent of the visitors to Turkey? To make matters worse, we had arrived in Istanbul on the same day that the U.S. military had moved into Baghdad. Perhaps it would be best to stay on the beaten path.

But Kat and I are both stubborn. The best way to get us to go somewhere … is to tell us we shouldn't or can't.

That is how we found ourselves scrunched into the back seat of a troop truck between the towns of Hani and Leche in Southeastern Turkey.

At the check point we were greeted by the senior officer who explained that the road we were attempting to cycle was closed to outside traffic. He opened up a map and showed us a couple of alternative roads to head east. After we had agreed to alter our route and accepted some small gifts from the commissary (Snickers bars and a bag of potato chips), we were free to pedal on.

But on to where? There would be no hotels or campgrounds on this road. And the open wheat fields were not conducive to wild camping.

Late in the evening as we crested one of the many rolling hills, from behind the barbed wire fence we heard a man's voice yell, "Would you like to be our guests?"

"Yes," I heard Kat yell from behind me.

Soon we were the guests of the on-site crew of a regional oil pumping station. Our main hosts were Nazim, the forty-seven-year-old Kurdish night watchman for the facility, and Deverim, a thirty-year-old Turkish engineer who had also worked in Saudi Arabia and Yemen.

We stayed up late talking about life, current politics and the Turkish-Kurdish conflict. Nazim and Deverim are good friends despite the ethnic conflict. The students throughout Turkey are taught in Turkish, even in areas that are one hundred percent Kurdish.

"Language is important to a culture," Nazim told us. "Yet I cannot speak to my daughter in my native tongue. She doesn't want to speak it."

They both believed the war in Iraq was about oil, as did most of the people in Turkey we spoke to. Yet we were never treated badly when we admitted to being Americans, even when our hosts were angry with our government.

Our space on the floor of one of the spare trailers on the compound was a far cry from the bedroom with a view of the Aegean Sea we'd had on the west coast, but there we had been tourists and here we were honored guests.

This mostly overlooked region of Turkey was fascinating travel … but it was not easy travel.

I am not afraid of dogs, but the Kangal dog of Turkey, an ancient flock-guarding breed, weighs from ninety to 140 pounds. When one of those dogs runs, no, gallops toward you, you may lose control of your bladder. I discovered though, that if I stood on my pedals while screaming and barking (yes, I said barking) as loudly as possible, I could become the alpha Kangal dog of eastern Turkey. And, believe me, you do not want to be the beta dog in this situation.

We often longed for the cute cafés that we encountered in western Turkey as we cycled through long barren stretches in the east.

In one Kurdish town we searched high and low for a place to stay, only to discover that the one hotel was connected to the police station. The price they quoted us for a room was so high that we had to stifle our laughter.

Yet four kilometers outside this town was an abandoned tourist site with ancient caves carved out of the mountainside. We pitched our tent under the stars and fell asleep to the sound of a large herd of goats and sheep high up the hillside. The Kurdish shepherd visited our campsite in the morning and we fixed him a cup of tea. He was so pleased with our simple gift that he grabbed one of his large ewes and milked her right into our cook pot.

On one of the many small roads we traveled, we were trying to find something to eat at a tiny roadside store. We were tired of eggs and pasta cooked over our camp-stove. A man approached us and asked where we were from. We told him and he invited us to his sister's place for some chai. We waited outside while she set the table. Forty-five minutes later we walked into a feast: olives, bread, cheese, onions, basil and a baked dish that involved tomatoes and eggplant that I still dream about. Over fifteen people filled the room and we all ate off a communal plate. Kat and I left with a bag of bread and cheese for the road.

In another town we were taken in by Zana, a schoolteacher. He was in this village as part of his national service. Zana gathered his fellow teachers and we all drove out to the lake for a late-night fish dinner. We stayed up late into the night talking with him about his dreams to open up a travel agency devoted to eastern Turkey, promoting places that the Turkish government doesn't talk about.

"I am bored in this small town," he confided. "I am surrounded by people, even my closest friends in this room, who are not interested to look beyond this village to the grand world out there."

With no hotels or hostels to speak of, each night it was a different cultural exchange. One evening we camped next to a military lookout tower. The soldiers invited us for chai and the sergeant tried to teach me to chant the evening Muslim prayer. I never got it right, but we all laughed ourselves silly.

We cycled further and further east, pedaling around Lake Van, Turkey's largest lake, it's green-blue waters so alkaline that you can wash your clothes in it without the aid of soap.

We left the beautiful shores of Van and pedaled northeast towards Iran. The road was hot, dusty and dry and as we climbed into the mountains it became cold, windy and dry. Little boys threw rocks at us. Not in a threatening way, but annoying enough under the circumstances to dampen our spirits.

We wound up a mountain pass, mile after mile of steep climbing through an ancient lava flow. We later discovered that this was the highest paved pass in the country, yet our cartographers had failed to indicate it on our map.

We rested at the summit for a while and then began our descent. We turned the first corner and were hit with the most stunning view imaginable. There was Mt. Ararat; its snow capped peak looming over the world. I'm not sure I believe there was a Noah, but if I had an ark and the world's floodwaters were receding, that is where I would anchor.

The golden rays of a late summer's eve lit up the vast green valley below and the white spire of a mosque flashed in the distance. For ten miles we descended into sheer and absolute beauty as a tailwind gently pushed us along. It was the perfect descent. I smiled from ear to ear, tears ran down my cheeks as I laughed and every once and awhile called out to Kat, "Can you believe we're here?"

We traveled through Turkey for three months. The southeast took up three weeks of that journey. Yet most of the people, most of the impassioned conversations, most of the tears and much of the laughter that are etched in my memory are from the southeast.

You can have an adventure in western Turkey, but you will have to seek it out. In southeastern Turkey, adventure will find you … whether you like it or not.

YOU'LL BE STAYING ANOTHER NIGHT

THE MOST IMPORTANT piece of advice that I can give to someone heading out on an extended bicycle journey is ... don't over-plan. It is also the most difficult piece of advice to follow, especially for a first-time traveler.

Planning gives one a sense of security. It helps suppress hyperventilation and anxiety attacks prior to leaping off into an adventure. But stare at that map long enough and I guarantee you'll go too far.

The brilliant idea will come to you that if you average ninety-six miles a day, you'll be able to visit fifteen major national parks, six museums and still have time to catch the annual yellow zucchini festival. Or you'll alleviate all fear of not finding a place to stay by calling ahead and making reservations at thirty-four hotels and fifty-three campgrounds along your "carved-in-stone" route.

Adventures are many, many things ... but they are never planned. Trips are planned. Adventure is what happens when the plan takes a detour. But detours take time, and if you've planned your journey down to the fine minutia, there is little or no wiggle room for adventure to squeeze into.

I've learned this lesson many times, but one stands out. On my bicycle journey down through Mexico I met three Canadian travelers who were driving a Volkswagen camper van. We shared a couple of days and a campsite in the mountains of Chiapas.

"Wouldn't it be great if we could meet up in Guatemala?" someone mentioned in the combined brilliance of a full moon and a roaring campfire.

I hesitated at first, but promised I'd meet them in six days at noon in the central park of the old city of Antigua. I'd have to average about seventy-five miles a day over the mountains, but it was doable. They drove off the next morning,

"See you on Friday!" they called.

A couple of days later I crossed the border into Guatemala and in the first village I pedaled into I was instantly adopted by three charming Mayan sisters, all in their fifties. They fought over who would get to house the traveler. A compromise was reached and I ate dinner at one sister's house, stayed with the family of another, and had breakfast at the home of the third sister.

I was surrounded by mountains, parrots, laughter and hospitality and stuffed with homemade bread and fresh orange juice.

At breakfast, the husband of the eldest sister approached me and said that it would be an honor to show me their mountains. He was going up to check on some cattle—a three-day ride—and pointed to the horse he already had saddled for me.

It was just my luck. I had been pedaling for over four plan-free months and now the only plan I'd made was going to derail a magical adventure.

I explained to him in my poor Spanish that I had promised to meet some friends in just three days time, and couldn't accept his most generous offer.

Fast forward a year and a hemisphere to New Zealand. I was seated at the bar in a pub in Dunedin on the South Island. Over a pint, I got to talking to a fellow cyclist from England. He was headed back up the coast and then turning inland.

"Why don't we plan to meet up …"

I stopped him in mid-sentence.

"I'm trying to eliminate "plan" from my travel vocabulary. How about, "Maybe I'll see you and maybe I won't.""

He had enough of a wayward travelers attitude not to be offended.

The next day I pedaled into the town of Middlemarch in a drizzle. A group of men in Scottish garb were filing out of a meeting hall.

"You got a place to stay?" a man holding a bagpipe approached me. "My name's Neal and if you cycle down that road I'll meet you out by our driveway."

About twenty minutes later there was Neal out by his mailbox as he had promised.

He greeted me with, "You'll be staying another night. Tomorrow's New Year's Eve. That's no night to be alone in a tent now is it?"

Neal introduced me to his wife Wendy and his son Toby, age nine, and his daughter Megan, age six, before showing me to my cozy guest room in their beautiful 1917 farmhouse.

I had a feeling I'd remember this particular holiday. Boy was I right.

How many people can say they spent New Year's Eve touring around in a bus with a New Zealand highland pipe band? And not your average pipe band—this one was comprised of four bagpipes, two drums and two saxophones. But in a small town, you take what you can get.

The guys in the band were dressed to the hilt, or should I say kilt. They all looked authentic, except for those two saxophone players. I couldn't help calling them the "McBlues Brothers". The small school bus was driven by Wendy, chosen for her ability to drive a multi-passenger vehicle and willingness to drink soda without the Scotch.

The first stop was someone's garage. The handful of observers outnumbered the band, which assembled in a semi-circle around a table filled with munchies, beer and scotch. They blew out three or four numbers and then it was time to drink and chat.

The next stop was the golf course where only the proprietor was present. "One more than last year," someone commented.

The band played in the small ceramic tiled bar/clubhouse. A serious problem with bagpipes is their lack of volume control, so it was like being at a Celtic heavy metal concert. The audience of one took the time to take his fingers out of his ears and gave a round of hearty applause before handing round pitchers of beer and, yes, a bottle of scotch.

Wendy drove the band on to the Sun Club—a nudist camp. The members were all clothed. I'm not sure if it was out of sensitivity for their guests or because it was bloody cold outside. More tunes, more beer and more whiskey. The band actually appeared to be playing much better as the night went on. The president of the Sun Club gave them some extra money and requested Amazing Grace. She didn't have to pay though, because I believe a Scotsman is not allowed to turn down a request to play Amazing Grace (even if he's living in New Zealand).

Next stop—a private party: More tunes, more refreshments. Oh. And some trout. Very nice. By then, I was beginning to feel the urge to take off my clothes and play "Free Bird" on the pipes, but I remained the slightly tottering observer.

Last stop was the pub, where everybody in Middlemarch who wore clothes was drinking whiskey and beer. The band marched into the pub and squeezed their way into the back. It seemed to me they could have saved a lot of time and gas by simply playing at the pub all night.

At 11:59 PM, I asked the woman in front of me what they did at midnight. She put down her beer and free sausage (provided by the pub in gratitude for a month's worth of business in one night) and said, "Not much."

She was right. The band was halfway through "Auld Lang Syne" for the second time before anyone noticed we were in a new year.

At 2:30 AM as the bus rocked and bumped its way down farm roads, Neal leaned over and said, "You'll be staying another night."

"I've got no plans," I replied.

"Good. Because we've already bought you tickets to the races."

We spent New Year's Day picnicking at the horse races with, I'd swear, every family within a hundred miles.

It may not have compared to a Guatemalan mountain horse trek, but it felt great not to have to turn down genuine hospitality because of pre-made plans.

By the way. The year prior, when I arrived in Antigua, Guatemala at the promised time and location—my travel friends were nowhere to be found.

TO CATCH A THIEF

WHEN I WAS thirteen years old I got my first ten-speed. It was a yellow Vista Esquire with black trim. I rode it everywhere. The library. The store. To my old neighborhood. To Ancil Hoffman Park. And to school. Twice a day.

I began my seventh grade year taking the bus to school. But a gang of bullies had selected me as their favorite target, so I elected to ride my trusty yellow Vista Esquire. When it came time for lunch, I'd ride it home, eat a peanut butter and jelly sandwich or three and cycle back (the less time I spent at school, the smaller the window of opportunity for being bullied).

My bike was as faithful as a trusted dog, always at my side. I think I would have slept with it if my parents had allowed.

I remember the moment I lost my companion like it was yesterday. I had found a couple of old coins and I was sure they were worth thousands, if not millions of dollars. I parked my bike at the rack outside the Thrifty drugstore. I didn't lock it. Didn't need to. I was only going to peruse *Coin and Stamp Monthly* at the magazine counter, which was within sight of my parked bike.

I ran inside and within ninety seconds had located the year and mintmark of the nickels I'd found. They were worth a total of seventy-one cents. I quickly came to the realization that I could not cash out a millionaire and leave junior school behind. I ran towards the exit and by the time my foot hit the rubber pad that activated the automatic door, life, as I knew it, was over.

It was gone. A bike rack never looked so lonesome. Panicked looks in both directions spotted no fleeing thief.

It was a hard and brutal lesson. For years afterward, there wasn't a month that went by that I wouldn't dream of coming out of the drugstore and finding the thief in the midst of his crime. I was never Willie the pudgy junior high school student in my dream. I was Bruce Lee or Steve McQueen or John Wayne and the criminal always paid a high price for messing with my trusty steed. I always woke up as the thief begged, "I'm sorry. Please don't."

It's no doubt due to this personal trauma that my ears have always perked up around stories of theft.

I met a man named Kirk who had lived on his bicycle for over two years. Sold everything and went traveling. Every possession he had in the world was packed into the panniers of his mountain bike. He'd been all over the world without incident. Then he made the mistake of going into an all-you-can-eat salad bar in Santa Cruz, CA. He locked his bike to itself, and due to its substantial weight, he figured it was safe. He chose a seat near the window, but one that put his back to his bike.

On his way back from his sixth trip to the salad bar, he glanced out the window and saw an empty parking lot where his bike used to be. He ran out and followed the rubber streaks where the thieves had dragged his bike and hoisted it into a truck. He stood in the parking lot and realized, as he reached into his pocket, that the clothes he was wearing and thirty-seven cents were all he had left in the world.

I was once in a hotel lobby in Costa Rica checking into a low budget room. The couple in front of me was filling out their registration when a man walked up and announced, "Were those your backpacks by the door? A man just left with them." They ran out into the street and I followed in close pursuit. All three of us scanned the streets with no sign of their backpacks or a thief. When we returned to the lobby, it was only then that we realized that it was the Good Samaritan that had been the thief. He had simply placed the packs out of the way and when we ran out the entrance, he left with their bags out another exit.

In Mexico I met a German cyclist—a giant of a man who stood at seven feet nine inches. He traveled with a basketball bungee-corded to his back rack. He had been on the road for eleven months and taken thousands of photos. He was paranoid of losing his film in the mail, so he kept it all with him. One afternoon we came back from a brief swim in the ocean. He cursed in English, Italian, German and French. His right front pannier was gone ... and with it seventy-eight roles of undeveloped film.

No matter what the scenario, I always imagined what it would be like if I could have caught the thief. If only I had been wary enough to have stayed in the lobby in Costa Rica and confronted the con-artist crook:

"Nice try, my friend." I would have said with a wry smile. "Ply your dishonest trade elsewhere."

How grand to have come in from the sea a few minutes earlier, just in time to chase down the beach bandito hauling my German friend's memories away in a sack. What shear pleasure to present Kirk with his beloved bike and all his possessions after I had apprehended the crooks.

And if only I had spent just thirty seconds less in that drugstore when I was thirteen. But it was always "should have, could have, would have." I had to face the facts, as far as my life experience summed it up ... crime paid.

After a five-month journey in India, during which I managed only to lose a couple of water bottles to village kids who just couldn't resist the temptation, I was flying home and had a layover in Amsterdam.

Skipol Airport is a hustling, bustling hub of European travel. I had retrieved my bike and panniers from my KLM flight and took the elevator down to the floor below to check on my connecting flight with Northwest Airlines. I was in no hurry and was enjoying listening to the many languages being spoken by scurrying travelers.

As I waited in line, my eye caught a man walking briskly with a briefcase. Something was odd, though. Every two or three seconds he glanced behind himself with a nervous jerk of his head. Then I noticed a man in a business suit, about 300 feet behind him, running.

He yelled out, "Stop that man! He's a thief!"

Everyone looked up: travelers, booking agents, rental car personnel, janitorial staff. No one did anything. It was as if we were all extras in the filming of a TV show. Then someone broke out running after the thief. It happened so quickly and without thought, that it took a couple of seconds for it to register … it was me.

I'd let my bike fall to the ground and I felt my quads that had over 5,000 miles of training, surge into action. By the time I reached the bottom of the escalator, the thief was at the top. I took the steps three at a time and quickly closed the gap between us. The thief was as surprised at being pursued as I was shocked at being the pursuer. He let go of the briefcase and it clattered to the floor. He made a dash for the revolving doors that led out of the building, but just before he made his escape, I caught him and put him in a full nelson or some other amateur wrestling hold.

The airport security were there within seconds and took over. They handcuffed the suspect and gathered up the suitcase he'd been fleeing with.

As I rode the escalator back down to retrieve my bike, everyone looked up again. But this time there was applause. Not screaming and yelling like at a football game. But polite clapping and big smiles, as if I'd just sunk a birdie on the sixteenth hole, or managed not to trip a gate at an equestrian event.

One of the security guards asked, "What were you thinking? That could have been extremely dangerous. We are not allowed to pursue in this type of scenario."

"I don't know," I replied.

But that wasn't true. What my insides had been screaming throughout the whole affair? "I don't know who you are or where you live now, but this is for stealing my yellow Vista Esquire."

A FISH STORY

I CAN'T REMEMBER when the habit began, but it is now a hard and fast rule of the road. When ordering at a restaurant or café or bar or street-side stall where no prices are posted, I always ask "How much?" before I begin eating. Because once you've taken that first bite, you're committed. And if you haven't established a price—the skies the limit.

Kat and I cycled up a long winding mountain pass in Macedonia. The prior two months of cycling up and down the many mountain passes of Romania and Bulgaria had more than prepared us for this climb.

Many people had warned us about the scarcity of food in Eastern Europe. But we had found bakeries with dense brown loaves of bread the size of truck tires, fresh honey provided by beekeepers, and produce markets heaped with cucumbers, tomatoes, peppers and onions. And to top it off, it was all incredibly inexpensive thanks to the generous exchange rates at the time. I'd never eaten better or felt healthier.

At the top of the pass, an icy wind forced us to put on our rain jackets under blue skies. We stood and looked out over Lake Ohrid—considered to be one of the oldest and deepest lakes in Europe.

On the other side of the enormous lake lay Albania, the final country in our Balkans adventure. A country so closed off from the rest of the world that I had yet to meet someone who had ever traveled there.

We coasted down the other side of the pass, winding our way toward the shores of Lake Ohrid. We pulled into the first village we encountered to thaw out our numb fingers and toes.

Several kids surrounded our bikes and a man with jet-black hair, wearing a thick wool sweater caught our eyes and asked, "Coffee?"

We left our bikes at a little shop and followed our host down some steep steps toward the lake. We walked onto a patio of what appeared to be a small informal restaurant. The man gestured for us to sit down at a modest wooden table and soon after he brought us tiny cups of sweet, black coffee.

The scene was idyllic. Huddled with our cups of coffee, protected from the icy wind by sturdy stone walls, we listened to the waves lap against the smooth pebbled beach.

On the other side of the patio an old woman was stoking the fire under an outdoor stove. A large fish was sizzling away on top of the grill. Our host asked us, "You like?"

"Sure," we both said. We hadn't seen a menu. But how much could it cost? Our most expensive meal so far at a nice restaurant in Macedonia had come to six dollars, including a bottle of wine.

Our host transformed into our waiter and we were served up the entire fish and a mound of fried potatoes.

It was pretty good. Not anywhere near the best food we'd eaten in the Balkans, but the surroundings and our good moods transformed it into a spectacular dining experience.

After we had eaten every speck of food on our plates, our waiter handed me a slip of paper.

I stared at the bill. There had to be a mistake. The amount of Macedonian denars circled at the bottom of the slip of paper translated to thirty-five dollars. Considering what we had been paying for meals in Macedonia, Romania and Bulgaria, the total was the equivalent of walking into McDonalds and being charged $112 for a Big Mac—without fries.

I called the man over and motioned for him to add up the bill again. A few moments later he assured me with a nod that his math was correct.

Then it hit me. I hadn't asked. I had broken my own travel rule and now I was going to pay for it, dearly.

I glanced up at the man waiting for his exorbitant fee. He had me. The glib look on his unshaven face broadcast it. I employed him to check his math again, but he shook his shoulders and pointed down at the bill.

A dislike—no—a hatred for this man began to well up in me. He had greeted us with a smile and open arms, only to lead us down to this den of thievery. But I wasn't going to go down without a fight.

"Owner," I yelled. "I want to see the owner. The chief. The head dude."

The man apparently understood some my English, because he pointed up to the hill. I grabbed the bill and motioned for him to follow me and marched off.

I stomped up the cobbled streets with a confident, determined gate, checking back to see if I was heading in the right direction. Our waiter followed sheepishly behind, pointing up to a small house.

When the owner finds out how much his employee is charging us for fish and chips, the price would surely plummet, I thought. We might even get it for free with sincere apologies. Our waiter looked more and more concerned. My confidence grew.

We arrived at what I discovered was another small restaurant. Our waiter disappeared inside and soon a handsome man in his thirties with a clean white shirt and a tie walked out.

I thrust the bill in his hand and pointed at the total and then pointed accusingly at the waiter.

The owner looked at the bill awhile and then said in English, "This price is fare. Thirty-five dollars."

The veins in my head began to swell. "So this is a village full of thieves," I ranted. I reached for my wallet. "OK. OK. You want thirty-five dollars for fish and some greasy potatoes. Here."

I pulled out the money and in a grand gesture, making sure everyone who had now gathered saw my actions, I threw the bills down on the ground at his feet. "I hope you choke on it," I declared.

Every face, including the owner's, registered absolute disbelief. I turned and marched down the hill, stopping a few times to glare back at the owner. Kat had already gathered our bags and was back at the bicycles.

"Let's get out of here," I grumbled.

The beautiful waters of Lake Ohrid, and my opinion of Macedonia had been tarnished. Wasn't it a shame that the actions of a few could ruin what could have been the perfect day? My tantrum had drained some of my rage. It had been worth making a scene to know the restaurant owner might contemplate long and hard before pulling that scam on another traveler. I felt the warm glow of righteous indignation.

Until we pedaled into the resort town of Ohrid.

There in the windows of every restaurant were signs in English and German. A wave of embarrassment and downright shame washed over me. Each and every sign, in large block letters, identified Willie Weir as the ugliest of ugly Americans.

"Special Lake Ohrid Trout—A delicacy—$35."

GIMME SHELTER

THERE IS A simple item that has allowed me to travel the world. It has no motor and its design has changed very little over time. It has had such an impact on my life that it was included in a song sung at my wedding.

It is not the bicycle, but the humble and simple accommodation in a stuff sack—the tent.

I can't remember the first night I slept in a tent. It might have been in my childhood buddy Vernon Heffner's back yard or on a Cub Scout trip, or possibly with my father on an Indian Guides outing outside of suburban Sacramento, CA.

But whenever it was, there was something magical about arriving in a foreign space and in a matter of minutes having a safe haven. You were safe from bugs and bears (at least I thought I was back then) and all things wild. Then, after a good or horrible night's sleep, you packed it all up and (if executed correctly) looked back and saw no signs of you ever having been there.

It wasn't until my first bicycle trip across the United States, however, that I spent more than a couple of consecutive nights in a tent. I bought a ninety-nine dollar free-standing tent that I ended up using for the next decade. When it finally wore out, I bought a little yellow freestanding tent at REI for ... ninety-nine dollars.

I mostly traveled alone with that tent. The extra room allowed me to bring my bicycle inside. And when I met my life's partner, Kat, it was a symbolic moment when I invited her inside—"Welcome to my safe haven and a life of adventure."

Kat and I prefer to call it our hamster's nest. For once we've unpacked all our gear, laid out our mattresses and sleeping bags, and piled up our panniers inside, there appears to only be enough room for a couple of small rodents. We happily burrow inside, stuffing all our extra clothing into stuff-sack pillows.

What I find fascinating is how safe and secure I feel, even as an adult, in this dwelling of nylon, mesh and zippers. Every time I enter my fragile dwelling it becomes my castle, my fort, my headquarters and I'm somehow eight years old again.

This feeling often lasts until morning when reality sets deeply into my lower back and hips. I exit an old man, hunched over and groaning. The morning creaks and groans were with me in my twenties, but after a couple of minutes I was back to normal and ready to eat breakfast and face the day. Now that I'm in my forties, I find it harder to transition out of tent posture and often remain hunched over through breakfast and breaking camp where it slowly merges with bike posture.

I'll be honest and admit that my camping days would have been over a decade ago were it not for two items—the Therm-a-Rest mattress and the small fabric camp chair.

And my camping days can't be over, because then my life as an adventure cyclist would be over as well.

I realize that there are many people who travel by bicycle who do not and will not do the camping thing. That's OK. There are plenty of people who have the exact same relationship with their credit card that I have with my tent. It is a small item that allows them to travel by bicycle.

But my small annual income does not allow me a "for everything else there's MasterCard" weekend, let alone a five-month journey. The tent provides me with two travel essentials—flexibility and frugality.

The tent is the great budget equalizer of a journey. When you are traveling in a country that has inexpensive hotels and accommodations, you can leave the tent stuffed in your panniers for weeks. But as the prices go up for inns and hostels, so can the number of days you spend in your tent.

Without a tent, the difference between a two-month journey in Denmark and Mexico would be thousands of dollars. With a tent and camping always as an option, the difference in dollars spent would be hundreds not thousands.

If I had gone to South Africa without a tent and stayed in hotels my budget would have covered a trip of about three weeks. With a tent my money lasted five months! Talk about a dollar-stretcher.

A tent can come in handy even when you are not camping. I once stayed in a cheap hotel in southern Mexico. The mosquitoes came in clouds as thick as London fog and they were vicious. This less-than-stellar accommodation had no screens and I had no mosquito net. It was so hot outside that closing my hotel room door would have meant death by asphyxiation. There was a four-star hotel down the street, but the cost of one night would set me back two weeks travel budget. I pondered my predicament while swatting at the little flying Draculas, smashing their little bodies up against the walls and the low ceiling.

I finally realized that my only option was to set up my tent on top of my hotel bed. I centered my little yellow tent on the mattress and it hung over on either side. It was actually quite comfortable. The look the hotel owner gave me when she came to the room to collect my payment was priceless. I promised her I wouldn't use my camp stove or dig a pit toilet in the floor and she laughed until tears welled up in her eyes.

A tent allows you the luxury of not planning. Your trip can be completely flexible because you don't have any reservations to book, deposits to lose, or schedules to keep.

If you're prepared to camp and you knock on some farmer's door in South Dakota, South America or South Africa, your potential host has options. They can give you permission to camp on their property or they can invite you in to stay in their guest room.

Nowhere did the value of traveling with a tent become more apparent than in Cuba. I traveled first in the western province of Pinar del Rio for two weeks. This area is very touristy and I never found a place to camp. When Kat joined me in Havana, I decided to leave the tent behind at our hotel.

Two days out, I knew I'd made a mistake. We could always find accommodation in the large cities and towns, but in the smaller villages, people literally didn't know what to do with us. Most Cubans live in modest homes with very little room to spare—but there were plenty of places to camp.

Before we headed off on a loop along the undeveloped coastline between Pilon and the city of Santiago, I took an overnight train back to Havana and picked up our tent.

The sixteen hours on the train were worth it. With the flexibility of carrying our own lodging we had entire pristine beaches to ourselves and didn't worry about whether or not we'd make it to the next town. We also were invited to stay and camp on the property of locals. They didn't have a spare bed in the house, but they were delighted to have foreign guests in their garden.

I understand that the older I get, the more uncomfortable my chosen travel method will become. But I will pedal my bicycle around this planet for as long as my legs hold out. And I will sleep in a tent for as long as my hips and back will allow it. For when it comes to travel, the bicycle and the tent are a perfect match.

IT'S ABOUT TIME

"Now David's a carpenter that's his life's trade.
And Willie does anything, long as he's paid.
But both of them like to pedal up hills,
And don't care for luxury, money and frills."

TWO CYCLISTS SANG out made-up refrains to the tune of an old folk song as they pedaled along an "improved" road near the edge of the Sawtooth National Forest in southeastern Idaho.

I met Dave Maynard as a fellow actor in a low-budget Seattle production of "Babes in Toyland" in 1985. The theatre we were working for went bankrupt mid-production, and we performed the holiday show on a blank stage without a set.

We quickly discovered that we not only had theatre in common, but also bicycle touring.

"We should do a trip together sometime."

It took twenty years, but we'd finally managed it.

We pulled into Twin Falls, Idaho with our bikes in Dave's work van, an old Toyota with "Cotswold Carpentry" stenciled on the side. We needed to find a place to park the vehicle for a couple of weeks and asked the advice of an officer in a patrol car.

"That's not my department. Try City Hall," he told us.

I looked at our map and saw the little town of Hollister (population 138) about twenty miles south of Twin Falls.

"Why don't we start our journey there? My bet is that we won't be talking to a department; we'll be talking to "Bob" or "Fred".

Actually, it ended up being "Paul," the manager of the gas station/mini-mart/liquor store in Hollister.

"Sure. You can park your vehicle in the back of the lot. We'll look after it. With the price of gasoline the way it is, if you don't have a locking gas cap, I can't guarantee it'll have gas in it," he added with a chuckle. Then he put four fresh peaches from the shelf in a paper bag and handed them to me. "No charge. Have a good trip."

Dave and I pedaled a quarter mile down Highway 93, turned onto a small road that passed by the "Nat-Soo-Pah" hot springs and trailer camp, and then said goodbye to pavement as the road transitioned into "improved gravel."

Any cyclist who has traveled an "improved gravel road" knows that in reality this designation means, "Gravel has recently been dumped on this surface in order to make your life as a touring cyclist less than pleasant."

But the sun was out, the wind was at our backs, nary a cloud in the sky ... it was time to sing another chorus.

Sawtooth National Forest is not a large contiguous piece of land; it looks more like pieces of a broken plate scattered over the Idaho map. Dave and I would spend the next ten days riding through several "divisions" of the forest separated by farmland and Bureau of Land Management grazing land.

Not long after pedaling out of Hollister, we climbed up into the Cassia Division of the forest as the temperature climbed into the nineties. The unpaved road was no longer "improved" which suited us just fine. Within a half-mile stretch, we spotted Broad-tailed and Rufus Hummingbirds, followed by two Sandhill Cranes with their loud, frog-like calls. Within five minutes, we had managed to see the smallest and largest birds in the forest. The contrast was stunning. Almost as stunning as the contrast in temperature we experienced. The high on our first day of riding was ninety-three degrees. The high the very next day was forty-six as a cold drizzle set into the region.

We pulled our soggy selves onto the porch of an unoccupied ranger station, stripped off our wet clothes and fired up our stove to boil water for coffee.

A young ranger drove up in his truck and informed us that on August 16, this was the first rain of the summer. He seemed surprised to see a couple of old guys (anyone over thirty) traveling by bike. He was used to seeing hunters on ATVs and in campers hauling big trailers.

"The hiking trails are in bad shape because all the money goes into improving the bathrooms at the campgrounds," he said with disgust.

That evening the rains subsided and we pulled our bikes up to the top of a ridge and found a perfect wild campsite nestled among the pines and aspens. We lit a fire, watched the sunset, and told stories late into the evening.

There was a third member of our party, at least in spirit. Shorty Huber.

Shorty was Dave's grandfather. He was born in 1906 and began cycling when he was sixty-five years old. He and Dave cycled from their hometown of Helena, Montana across the country to Washington, DC in 1976. When people asked Shorty (who stood five feet two inches tall) why he liked to ride a bicycle his typical answer was, "Cause it feels so good when you get off."

He was cycling across the country "to demonstrate to people that they didn't have to burn up a bunch of oil to have a good time."

In 1984 they cycled New Zealand together. Shorty was quick to get frustrated with the bad weather or road conditions and had a tendency to forget the names of people they'd just met or places they'd just cycled through. "But he was seventy-eight years old!" Dave exclaimed. "He was always a travel companion and friend. An equal. It was easy to forget how old he was."

Six years later, Dave was planning yet another bicycle trip with his grandpa when Shorty was hit by a car and killed on his bicycle in Helena. Dave has a small metal plate attached on the frame of his mountain bike that reads, "This bike belongs to G.W. 'Shorty' Huber." Dave pried it off of the mangled wreck of his grandpa's bike and proudly travels with it.

The next afternoon we were chased down from the mountains into the little town of Oakley by a thunderstorm and managed to duck into a bar/restaurant before the skies opened up.

We bellied up to the bar and ate bacon double cheeseburgers while the locals inquired about our trip.

One old rancher with rotting teeth and wearing a shirt that hadn't been washed since the Carter administration stated,

"You going to the City of Rocks? That place was all but ruined when they made it a national reserve. Used to be able to go in there and do whatever you wanted."

After we stocked up at the tiny grocery store and had a chocolate-peanut butter shake at the gas station/snack shop, we pedaled south-east toward the reserve.

We pedaled in from the west, crested the summit, and the valley opened up. We stood in awe and I thought, "Why have I never heard of this place?"

The "City of Rocks" is just that—a valley filled with clusters of granite seemingly rising out of the earth. It was a landmark for the pioneers traveling along the California Trail. Today it is a destination for rock climbers around the world.

We found an idyllic "walk-in" campsite buffeted by granite, mountain mahogany and pinyon pine.

The best way to see the City of Rocks National Reserve is on foot, so Dave and I left our bikes at our campsite and did a couple of day hikes. With names like Banana Rock, Upper Breadloaves and Beef Jello Rock, I got the distinct feeling that these granite towers had been named by climbers in VW campers, not pioneers on wagons.

Thunderstorms loomed on the outskirts of the park, but we stayed dry and were treated to a full moon rising from our own granite perch above our campsite.

In the morning I was packed up before Dave and told him I'd meet him at the hand water pump out by the road. Dave is still using his grandpa's fabric panniers, which require him to double bag anything and everything. I kept waiting for the panniers to melt off his bike when it rained. He showed up forty-five minutes later.

"I was having some grandpa moments. Sorry it took so long. I was always waiting for Shorty. Now I'm the slow one."

"Don't worry, Dave", I said. "We all get to be grandpa at one time or another."

The headquarters for the City of Rocks is in the nearby town of Elba. Thanks to the constant flow of climbers in desperate need for a pizza or a hamburger and a microbrew, the town sports a great café, but not much else. The only store was pitiful. Why wasn't there more retail?

I got my answer in overhearing an exchange with a five year-old girl and her mother. They were at the visitor center and the mother picked up an item and carried it to the counter. The little girl grabbed her mom's arm, "Don't Mommy. You can get the same thing at WalMart for half the price."

Sigh.

Back on the flats again, we made good time and stopped near a creek to wash out our clothes. (We knew that our entire trip would be sans showers or laundry facilities). We cycled into the Raft River Division of the Sawtooth and quickly discovered we had arrived on the first day of bow-hunting season.

If I'm going to pedal anywhere during hunting season, I'll take bow hunters over your average hunter with a gun any day. Bow hunting is quieter by a couple hundred decibels. Arrows are expensive enough that hunters don't shoot them indiscriminately. And bow-hunting takes enough skill that hunters rarely knock back a couple of six packs before looking for something to kill.

A father and his young son and daughter approached us on their ATVs. They were all dressed in camo overalls and all were no less than forty pounds overweight. "Where the hell are you going?" the father asked.

"One Mile Canyon."

"You'll never make it!" he stated.

When we reached the incredibly steep climb the next morning and finally walked our bikes up the last stretch, we knew what he had been referring to.

Back out of the mountains and back onto the plains, we were running low on foodstuffs—but no worries. We'd be pedaling through at least three towns.

One closed diner and two ghost towns later, we had a problem. We had at least three more days of riding and nowhere near the calories needed in our panniers. We were running out of water, but we had a pump and weren't worried of dying of thirst.

After a long, hot stretch through fallow fields we stopped and knocked on a farmer's door. We were greeted by Charlie, the dog, first and then by Gordon, a Mormon farmer who had raised seven children in his grandfather's home.

He invited us in, filled our water bottles. Then we all retired under the shade of a tree out in the yard. We sat out there for over an hour, talking local and world politics, while Charlie got his belly rubbed.

Gordon told us the story of struggling on the farm with seven small children. One year he hadn't even harvested ten percent of his wheat when a hailstorm came through and cleaned him out. He would lose his family's farm, for sure. He was devastated.

Later in the month, when he went to get his grain check, he looked down and it was made out for the same amount he'd received the year before. Impossible.

Each of his neighbors, without telling him, had taken a percentage of their harvest and put it in under his name.

"They knew I wouldn't accept it, so they kept it a secret. That's what true neighbors do for each other."

We all got teary-eyed as we sat outside the old farmhouse with its worn out steps and peeling paint.

As we got onto our bikes, Charlie's wife came out of the house and without a word, offered us a couple of cheese sandwiches.

We waved goodbye and both Dave and I immediately knew what the other was thinking. "That right there is why I choose to travel the way I do."

We still needed a store and agreed to go out of our way to the thriving metropolis of Malad City (population 2,117). It would end up being a sixty mile round trip over a 2,000 foot mountain pass, but we arrived back onto our route with panniers loaded with food and pedaled into the Curlew National Grasslands.

From there we ventured with compass and map along the Hudspeth cutoff. In 1849 this route supposedly saved over a hundred miles over the California Trail. Although that wasn't the case (it saved maybe twenty and actually took longer) over 40,000 people traveled this route.

Over 150 years later a couple of cyclists followed the same tracks through lonely grasslands. We realized we hadn't seen a person or vehicle the entire day.

We had to get permission to cross a farmer's wheat field and then pedaled through Crazy Canyon up to the Sublett Division.

In a familiar pattern, we camped in the hills and coasted down to the flats, pedaled across the valley and headed up into the mountains again (Albion Mountain Division).

We pulled back into the gas station/mini-mart/liquor store in Hollister ten days after we'd left.

"It's about time you got back," Paul the manager called out.

Dave and I had talked and spent more time with each other in those ten days than in the entire twenty years prior.

"How would you rate the trip?" I asked Dave.

He smiled. "Shorty would have approved."

MILES TO MEMORIES

Tᴉᴄᴋ. Tɪᴄᴋ. Tɪᴄᴋ. Tick.

That was the sound of bicycle travel when I was a kid. I saved up enough money to buy an odometer for my bicycle when I was twelve. The mostly plastic device was attached with clamps down toward the bottom of my right-front fork. A metal striker, attached to one of the spokes of my front wheel, needed to be lined up perfectly to strike the star-shaped cog of the odometer.

Tick. Tick. Tick. Tick.

That was the glorious sound of distance. Of miles. Of adventure.

The odometer sported three black dials for miles and one red one for tenths of miles—allowing me to travel a seemingly impossible 999.9 miles before it turned over.

Of course, on many occasions (usually on a downhill) the sound turned to, Tick, Boink, Thud, Thud, Thud, as the striker slipped and careened into the body of the odometer. I would slam on my breaks, hoping to bring my Schwinn three-speed to a dead stop before the odometer disintegrated. Then I would sit on the side of the road, for as long as it took, to realign that striker. I wasn't about to pedal one tenth of a mile that wouldn't be counted.

In junior high school I upgraded to my first ten-speed. But due to my obsession, I was more excited about my odometer upgrade.

Now I had the latest in distance tracking technology—a silent running odometer that ran off of a tiny rubber belt. No longer was I depressed going up a steep hill, listening for that "tick" indicating one wheel revolution.

But to my horror, I discovered that when the belt stretched and wore out, it stopped turning that wheel. I would gaze at the dial while coasting down a hill and discover it not registering. Again, I slammed on the brakes. How long had it not been functioning? How much of my day's pedaling had been in vain? How many precious miles uncounted? I found myself estimating the distance lost and then standing in our garage, my bike propped up, painstakingly spinning my front wheel for hours, as my fingers blistered, to recapture the lost miles.

By the time I pedaled across the U.S. on a bona fide touring bike, technology had rewarded me a "cyclo-coumputer". It must have weighed a couple of pounds including the batteries, but the fact that it could register my top speed AND my daily mileage, easily made up for its bulk.

My buddy Thomas and I set out to conquer the country—mile by mile. Afterwards, if you had asked me, I could have told you in great detail of our accomplishments: Our total miles, average daily mileage, number of century days (one hundred or more miles). If you wanted to know what town we were in when we logged our 1,000[th] mile? I'd tell you from memory. 4,000[th]? I knew the exact spot in the road. I truly believe that if my odometer had malfunctioned, I would have left my bike and hitchhiked to the nearest city to buy a new one, rather than estimate such a precious piece of information.

I can't tell you exactly when my mile fixation waned. It was a gradual process. But I can trace its beginnings to Cadott, Wisconsin.

Thomas and I had taken a couple of wrong turns late in the afternoon and found ourselves surrounded by dusk and the potential of thunderstorms. We were nowhere near a campground. We pedaled into a little town and down a residential street. We chose one particular house because it "looked" friendly. The garden was well tended. People who are kind to plants are less likely to be mass murderers was our theory.

Our hesitant knock was answered by a tall, substantial man with three days' growth of beard—Fred Flintstone on a bad day.

"What do you want?" he grumbled.

"Hello, Sir," I replied. "My friend Thomas and I are cycling across the U.S. There is no place nearby to camp, and we were wondering if we could set our tent up on your lawn or possibly lay our sleeping bags out under your carport?"

I'll never forget his answer.

He turned his back and yelled into the house, "Hey, Millie. You want to take in a couple of bearded transients?"

With that we were whisked into the home and hospitality of Buster and Millie.

It was almost 10 PM, but Millie insisted that they were just fixing up something to eat. After showers and a couple of sandwiches and several glasses of soda, we gathered around the little organ in the living room and sang songs, accompanied by Millie's eighty-six year-old mother.

After midnight we were tucked into guest beds out on the screened porch.

We woke up the next morning to calls for breakfast from a smiling and newly shaved Buster. He had been out for days searching for a couple of lost hikers and just returned home when we knocked on his door.

We walked over to our bikes, only to discover that Millie had gotten into our panniers and washed all of our clothes. Our T-shirts and underwear lay neatly folded on top of our back racks.

After a breakfast of eggs and about a loaf and a half of toast we were ready to get back out on the road with new-found energy and totally clean wardrobes for the first time since Montana.

When Thomas and I returned to our homes in Sacramento, we ended up calling Buster and Millie on their anniversary, which had been mentioned in conversation sometime between the organ medley and Johnny Carson's monolog.

We kept in touch, and just so happens, Buster's marine unit was having a reunion in Sacramento the next spring. It was our turn to roll out the hospitality, and Buster and Millie had dinner with both of our families.

I graduated from college and moved to Seattle to pursue a career in theatre. In 1990, I was cast as an Equity guest artist to perform in *Voice of the Prairie* at the Madison Repertory Theatre in Wisconsin.

Buster and Millie made the long drive to Madison to see the play. The first play Buster had seen in his life.

When the show ended and the cast took our curtain call, I picked out a couple of smiling faces I never would have recognized except for a fortuitous knock on a door in a little town of Wisconsin.

Today, decades after my cross-country trip, I can no longer remember the once-so-important mileage stats. I can, however, remember in detail the Busters and Millies of our journey and every other journey since.

I still travel with a cyclometer, although it is often covered up by my map case. And I've found myself more often relieved than horrified when the battery goes dead. If there is an experience to be had, I don't care if I've pedaled a hundred miles, or two miles—it's time to call it a day.

For what began as an obsession with distance, slowly transformed into a passion for travel and the memories and relationships collected along the way.

BRAVADO

"LOOK AT ME. Look at me. Look at me."

I always smile when I see a kid standing on a diving board at a public pool, screaming his or her lungs out. The goal, of course, is to gain the attention of parents, friends, the lifeguard and anyone within a half a mile, because (as everyone knows) a perfectly executed belly flop has no value unless there are plenty of witnesses. I smile because I've been there, all shivers and goose bumps, demanding the world take notice. At seven years old, there was never a debate on whether this was appropriate behavior or not. I just kept yelling until all eyes were on me.

Life's rules get a little more complex as we age. I know very few people who dislike being acknowledged for their accomplishments. And yet, adults are not socially allowed to stand up and simply yell, "Look at me."

Adults find more subtle ways.

They drive fast red sports cars. They buy 7,000-square-foot houses. They wear diamonds on the soles of their shoes.

Or in my case, they travel around on a bike piled with lots of gear.

Oh sure, I pedal for many other reasons ... physical fitness, culture, curiosity, adventure. But I've got to admit the seven-year-old boy in me loves that people notice. I don't have to yell. I don't even have to whisper.

Any bicycle traveler is well aware that it is nigh near impossible to pedal into a public place with forty or fifty pounds of gear balanced on a non-motorized vehicle, without several people approaching and asking, "Where you come from?"

This is solicited. This is information requested. And I have the option of answering their question with ten words or 10,000. It all depends on my mood. How many adults get the opportunity to subtly sing their own praises?

If a sales rep lands a great account or a huge bonus, do you think he can walk through the parking lot of the Piggly Wiggly and have strangers stop and ask him to please explain the spring in his step? He might want to shout it to the world, but the reaction is likely to be similar to that of a paunchy man in his fifties wearing a Speedo while yelling, "Look at me!" from the high dive of a public pool.

A loaded touring bicycle is a rolling "high dive." There is nothing like having dozens of people each day state, "I could never do what you're doing." or "You've pedaled that thing *how* far?" or simply "*Oh ... my ... God*" to feed one's ego.

You'd think I'd get enough of it. Apparently not, because on the rare occasion when I'm separated from my bike on a tour, I often find a way to elicit praise. I'll ask the clerk in a store, "How long is that pass coming into town? I thought my legs would fall off." This is their cue to ask me about my exploits.

Sometimes on a long journey my ego gets built up so much my head is in danger of exploding. Enter the ego deflators. These are people that life puts across my path to remind me that I am the merest of mortals.

Before I left for India, all of my friends and acquaintances reminded me how brave and adventurous I was to bicycle the sub-continent. Ninety miles into my journey I met a sixty-five-year-old man who had been on the road for two and a half years and pedaled over 22,000 miles. He had just come from China where he had car-ried his bicycle over two mountain passes because of snow … after his broken legs mended.

In Bosnia, I didn't have to worry about running into any serious touring cyclists—there weren't any. Most people were impressed or shocked that I was traveling there (in 1996) let alone cycling the recently mine-cleared highways. Then I met a local on the side of the highway who was trying to fix a broken spoke on this single-speed. He spoke some English and explained that he had been cycling to see the World Cup, but had been turned back at the Bosnia/Croatia border 200 miles into his journey.

He asked me where I had traveled and I ran down the list of places in the world I'd pedaled. He was impressed. Then he hopped (literally) onto his bike and pedaled off. It was only then that I real-ized he only had one leg.

If you are looking to get your ego stroked, you need to avoid gatherings of cyclists. Sure you'll find comradeship and common interests. But when you mention your latest trip over the Rockies, it will not be met with awe, but with "You think the Rockies are hard? Try the highlands of Ubetchastan!"

Early on in my travel career and before I met Kat, I discovered that youth hostels or "backpackers" were great places to raise my self-esteem to dizzying heights. Here were establishments filled with adventurous English speaking (albeit, mostly as a second language) travelers and each and everyone had arrived by train, car or bus. I would always relish the moment in the kitchen or at the dinner table when someone would ask how long I'd been on the road and from where and then discover I'd pedaled. Instant celebrity.

It was with this knowledge and experience that I entered a hostel in Costa Rica. A small inn, packed with world travelers in the lush rain forests of Montevideo. No one saw me check in, so my mode of transportation was not known. At the dinner table were seated a couple from New Zealand. Four Germans. Three Italians. A South African. A Canadian and two beautiful coeds from Basil, Switzerland.

I cooked up rice and beans and joined the group in the eating area. They were talking politics and music. Almost thirty minutes had gone by and no one had asked me the correct leading question. So I decided to initiate the topic myself. I turned to the Canadian, a skinny, bearded man in his twenties and asked him where he'd come from.

"I started up around the Arctic Circle."

The two attractive Swiss women perked up their ears. This was not the way it was supposed to play out. He was supposed to say, "Vancouver" or "Took the bus out of Cleveland" and then ask, "How about you?"

He went back to eating his pasta.

Not much of a conversationalist.

I prodded him again with, "How long have you been on the road?"

"About fourteen months."

Now the entire room had his attention. Now I just had to swing the conversation to me and the stage would be mine.

"Did you travel by bus or train or did you mostly hitchhike?"

No matter what his answer was, I could counter with, "I find pedaling to be the best way to see the world."

He looked up from his bowl and matter-of-factly stated.

"No. I walked. How about you?"

There was a long, long pause, during which a seven-year-old boy climbed down the ladder of a diving board and with his head hung low, shuffled into the locker room.

"Never mind."

BRINGING IT HOME

I STRAINED UNDER the weight of my load as I looked up at the steep grade ahead of me. Maybe I shouldn't have tried to carry so much. And yet, almost two years into this adventure, you'd think I'd be in better shape. On the other hand, I've found that being "in shape" feels differently at forty-five than it did at twenty-five.

The top of the climb was in sight. Within minutes I had reached the summit. It was all flat from here to base camp.

I turned the corner and walked up the two stairs onto the porch while fumbling for my keys. I unlocked the door and with a grunt shrugged off my backpack that contained our twenty-pound Thanksgiving turkey and other items for our feast.

I often bicycle to the store, but a twenty-pound bird won't fit in a standard pannier and my stretched out bungee cords are unreliable on a fourteen percent grade hill. The bus doesn't run frequently enough and I'm too frugal to call a cab.

And our car ... well ...

Kat and I had decided to give up our car with the help of the Washington State Automotive Redistribution Program (it was stolen). Whisked right out of our lives one sunny afternoon in March. It was an old, red all-purpose Subaru GL Wagon with four-wheel drive and just enough room for the two of us to sleep in the back.

This was fortuitous for me, because I had often pondered giving up on car ownership. Now I didn't have to get rid of our car ... I just had to lobby not to replace it.

I fixed Kat a drink and proceeded to make my case.

"The most amazing, enriching, enlightening times of our lives have been while bicycle touring in countries around the globe. Like many touring cyclists we relish the simplicity of the bicycle travel experience. We're always amazed how few possessions we need to make us happy. So why not try and live without a car, just as we travel without a car? What do you say?"

Kat looked up at me and said, "You arranged the theft, didn't you?"

"The key is to think of this not as a massive inconvenience, but as a grand adventure," I countered.

Kat didn't smile.

"OK. Maybe not a grand adventure," I conceded.

After much discussion we agreed to try it for a year.

Giving up your only car in the United States of American is not easy, even in Seattle, Washington.

Seattle has lots of bikes (and the largest bike club in America). It also has lots of hills and lots of rain.

In the wet winter months, or wet summer months, it is often best to be multimodal. To bike and bus, or to walk and bus.

But walking or biking or busing often takes a lot more time to cover the same distance than driving. Busses can be late. Feet can get tired.

The biggest adjustment was a mental one. It was discovering how interchangeable the words "adventure" and "hassle" can be.

Loading up my touring bike with all kinds of gear and food is an adventure.

Loading up my bike (or backpack) with groceries is a hassle.

Pouring over maps to find the best cycling route through Romania is an adventure.

Pouring over bike maps and bus schedules to find the best route to Renton is a hassle.

Arriving at a restaurant on a bike journey in wet soggy cycling clothes is an adventure.

Meeting friends at a local restaurant in those same soggy cycling clothes is a hassle.

We too often romanticize our travels while trivializing our daily lives.

Once we began to live our daily lives through the eyes of a traveler, the hassles transitioned into adventures.

The number thirty-six bus into downtown Seattle runs every ten minutes from our neighborhood of Beacon Hill. Through the eyes of a commuter it is a crowded, slow moving container of steel occupied by people wearing too much cologne or too little deodorant.

Through the eyes of a traveler it is a fascinating mix of humanity that runs the socio-economic gamut. Kat has counted over eight languages spoken on one trip to downtown. She delights in watching elderly Asian men and woman meeting up on their way to the International District. She's had conversations with people she would never otherwise meet socially. And when she returns home, there is always a story to tell.

I have an annual speaking engagement in Sequim, WA. It is sixty-eight miles away—a simple trip in a car. I figured it was impossible via public transportation. Then I contacted Mark Canizaro at the Bicycle Alliance of Washington. He has lived without a car for many years. He was able to email me a handout he'd created with the times and links to all the different transit agencies.

My trip to Sequim involved cycling from my house to the ferry dock on Seattle's waterfront. A thirty-minute ferry ride across Elliot Bay took me to Bainbridge Island. Waiting on the other side was the Kitsap County Transit bus number ninety, which took me and my bicycle to Poulsbo. Then it was a transfer to a Jefferson County Transit bus numer seven, which left me at "Four Corners" where I transferred to a number eight into Sequim. I took my bike off the rack and pedaled to the venue. The trip took three and a half hours and the total round-trip cost was twelve dollars and fifty cents.

What could be seen as a massive multimodal scheduling headache was, from a traveler's perspective, an exciting challenge. But do that trip every day and it becomes a hassle of epic proportions. Which is why giving up the car also changed our lifestyle.

We quickly began to shop, recreate and socialize closer to home. Our little neighborhood in the city of Seattle began to feel more like a village.

Because we walked and cycled much more, we began to discover the hidden gems of our neighborhood—the pocket parks, the gardens, the funky houses. The same sorts of discoveries we make in villages in other countries on our bicycle journeys.

We know more of our neighbors because we are outside more. We meet them walking to the bus stop or cycling to the grocery store.

And like a bicycle journey, our lives have become simpler. We don't buy the 144-roll package of toilet paper or 600 muffins at the warehouse store because getting it home isn't worth the effort. We don't schedule three different social engagements in one evening (like we did when we had a car) because we simply can't move that fast. So now we pick which events we truly want to attend. "Sorry, we don't have a car," is the perfect way out of an invitation you don't want to accept anyway.

To top it all off, it costs less, which allows us to save money for our next bicycle adventure.

Now I'm not saying that everyone needs to give up their car. There are plenty of places where it is simply impossible and plenty of professions that require one. What I'd like to suggest is to bring your adventures home.

The way you observe life on the road. The way you interact with people. The way you are in touch with the world and yourself when you are an adventurer ... bring it home. It doesn't have to end when you box up your bike or hang up your backpack at the end of a journey.

For within the heart and mind of an adventurer is a life of fewer hassles and more opportunities.

GO WITH THE FLOW

A DROP OF sweat fell from the tip of my nose onto the top tube of my bike. I could see the road curve sharply and steeply to the left. Stand and pedal for a hundred strokes. Sit for twenty. Repeat. Not this time. My legs gave out and I stopped, straddling my bike, my chest heaving in a wheezy attempt to fill my lungs with air.

It was time to walk. But I quickly discovered that this road was so steep, I didn't have the upper body strength to push my heavily loaded Rodriquez travel bike.

I looked back and there was Kat, 300 meters behind, struggling up the same grade. This is the kind of road that can be hard on relationships. Grades this steep can render all marriage vows null and void.

I put my head down on my front handlebar bag and waited for Kat to arrive. If she felt anything like I did at this moment, there were no words of encouragement in my repertoire worth uttering. Best to keep silent.

But, when I next looked up, she was straddling her bike beside me with a huge grin on her face. She was radiant, beaming. How could this be?

"What's up?" I asked.

In between gasps for air she said, "I just got a 'thumbs up' from a Buddhist monk."

Welcome to Thailand.

The route we were on is called the Mae Hong Son Loop or just "the loop," a 600-kilometer route that begins and ends in the city of Chiang Mai. With a quick glance at a map of northern Thailand, the loop entices many a traveler—a squiggly line that winds over mountains, through forest and parkland, flirts with the border of Burma, and then brings you back to where you began without retracing a single step.

With over 3,000 curves, this is a route that separates the tourists from the travelers. Highway 1095 from Chiang Mai to the town of Pai has so many sharp curves that regular tour buses don't even attempt it. Instead, an army of minivans shuttle travelers who occasionally lob toxic vomit bags out of the windows.

As a cyclist, it's not the curves that get you, but the grades. I've pedaled all over the world, and I haven't found anywhere that matches the consistent steepness of the roads of northern Thailand. It's as if the engineers were told they only had so much asphalt to work with.

But, for all the pain and agony, we were rewarded with a constant flow of praise and admiration. I have never experienced anything like it. The occupants of every van, car, truck and motorcycle cheered us on as if we were elite riders in the Tour de France. There were smiles, waves and shouts of encouragement, laughs of disbelief, and thumbs—hundreds of thumbs—pointing skyward in the internationally understood gesture of a job well done.

We couldn't wave back, our hands clutching the handlebars as sweat dripped off our noses and fingertips. But we acknowledged every one with a smile and a short nod of our heads.

Thailand charmed us from day one. Maybe it was the lack of expectations. We had heard so many stories of hordes of tourists. Our travel plans originally called for a two-week stint in Thailand before crossing over to Laos. Two weeks turned into seven.

Thailand has the three ingredients that make any country a pleasure in which to travel: friendly people, beautiful scenery, and incredible food.

The energy in Thailand beats to a different pulse than the rest of the world. Call it what you will. I like *chaotic bliss.*

It's capitalism with Buddhist undertones and a constitutional monarchy thrown in.

Reach the top of a mountain pass in northern Thailand and find an ancient Buddhist shrine *and* a Black Canyon Coffee outlet.

Eat the most deliciously fresh, spicy and aromatic phad thai from a streetside vendor, then walk into one of the thousands of 7-Eleven convenience stores and grab a Big Gulp if you wish.

Watch a Buddhist monk draped in saffron robes with modest sandals smoke a cigarette while shopping for DVDs in the local market.

Cycle through a traffic jam in Bangkok and you'll experience it as well: thousands of cars, buses, trucks and scooters idling in the middle of a muggy afternoon. Gridlock—no one honks, no one yells. To lose your temper in public is to lose face in Thailand. In the same scenario in New York or LA there would be bedlam and homicide.

In Thailand, both in traffic and in life, you learn to go with the flow.

One advantage of Thailand's popularity is the numerous affordable guesthouses you'll find in most towns and cities. For six to twelve dollars you can have a reasonably comfortable bed in a room with a fan and a shower.

No guesthouse at the end of the day? Pull over and ask to camp next to a police checkpoint or pedal up to a Buddhist monastery.

Three day's ride outside of Bangkok, Kat and I were watching the sunset over a flooded rice field when a woman drove up to us on a scooter and thrust a cell phone into my hand. The man on the line spoke a little English, and I finally surmised that we were being invited to stay—somewhere.

The woman pointed down the road, indicating which way we should pedal, and then proceeded to drive off in the opposite direction. We stood by our bikes in a state of confusion. She scooted back a minute later and explained that she was going to buy food.

Turned out that this woman was a teacher and her husband was the headmaster of the school. They hosted us in the teacher's lounge, spreading a feast out before us, including sweet-and-sour pork, tom yum soup, curries, and beef and long beans in oyster sauce.

I sat basking in the glow of a new international friendship and a second helping of curry. I knew the Thai word for delicious, so I got everyone's attention, gestured towards the many platters and announced with gusto, "Jung."

There was an awkward silence in the room as I sat with my spoon extended. Maybe I hadn't pronounced in correctly?

The husband was the first to crack, and he began to giggle. The custodian of the school, a Chinese woman, let out a huge cackling laugh, giving the polite crowd the opportunity to join in.

Kat leaned over and informed me that I had just complimented our host's dinner by announcing, "Mosquito."

So much for my international language skills.

The next morning, with the help of an interpreter, we spoke to over 300 students, followed by a command performance at another school across the river.

Our "go with the flow" route took us north out of Bangkok, through the flat rice basket of Thailand, taking time to visit the ancient cities of Ayutthaya and Kamphaeng Phet.

Then up into the foothills where elephants used to roam by the thousands. The elephant population in deforested Thailand is now under 2,000. Northwest of the city of Lampang, the Thai Elephant Conservation Center is well worth a visit.

Then on to Chiang Mai and the Mae Hon Son Loop. We returned to Chiang Mai, gathering with travelers from Canada, Australia, Germany and England for the Christmas holidays.

We spent days wandering around Chiang Mai, seeking out temples and markets and searching for the perfect bowl of *kow soy*, a spicy curry made with egg noodles and coconut milk.

We pedaled north of Chiang Mai, near the base of Doi Chiang Dao, Thailand's third highest mountain and up to the village of Mae Salong. The road to this Chinese Nationalist outpost was even steeper than the roads along the Mae Hong Son Loop. But the climb was worth it as we pedaled through the tea fields at 4,000 feet.

We screamed down from the mountains and aimed for Mae Chan, a little-visited Thai-Chinese town, for New Year's Eve.

We had spent Christmas with other travelers, so we wanted to spend New Year's Eve with locals. Mae Chan only had a couple of hotels, and one of them was completely booked. The owner looked embarrassed as she gave us directions to the only other hotel in town.

It ended up being a "love motel", a modest series of concrete rooms with carports with convenient "curtains" to pull in front of your car (or bicycles). We were issued our key, a bar of soap and a complimentary condom.

We left our bikes in our room and wandered through town. Although the Chinese New Year would be celebrated later in the year, the locals had set up a stage and the main street was lined with over sixty food booths.

We wandered through it all, the only westerners in town, sampling as much as our stomachs could hold.

On the way back to our hotel we strolled by a grand teak wood home: the grandest house in the city. A group was gathered outside for a party. They took one look at us and immediately waived us in to join them. We spent the rest of New Year's Eve laughing, eating and drinking with the wealthiest family in town. They were completely charmed that we would spend New Year's Eve with them.

We spent the next week cycling up north near the Myanmar border and then along the Mekong River to Chiang Kong, our crossing point into Laos.

If you want a gradual transition from the western world into Southeast Asia … Thailand is your ticket.

Every trip comes away with its defining moment. That place or event or person that represents what the journey was all about.

Kat and I were cycling out of the congested city of Chiang Mai to begin the Mae Hon Son Loop. Once a small town, this sprawling city is known now as the Bangkok of the north.

The traffic was heavy with cars, buses and scooters. Up ahead of us, an old man pedaled a single-speed bike. He wore loose-fitting trousers, a long sleeve shirt and a floppy hat. His knees shot out dramatically to the sides as he pedaled.

He turned to look behind him, probably to check traffic, and did a triple take. On his first glance he noticed a couple of cyclists. His second glance registered foreigners on loaded travel bikes. The third take was a longer one in which he noticed that one of the foreigners was a woman on a bicycle—and she was going to pass him.

A quick look of panic crossed his face. His head whipped back around, his shoulders hunched forward, and his thin little legs began pumping faster than I thought possible—his knees jutting out like pistons on a runaway train.

Kat took the bait and sped up, quickly closing in on the frantically pedaling old man. He was now glancing behind himself every three or four seconds, the look of panic growing more intense.

I thought, "Slow down, Kat. This poor man is going to die of a heart attack."

She finally pulled up alongside him, and I watched as the two them simultaneously looked at each other.

There was a brief stare-down, but what followed took me by absolute surprise. I couldn't see their faces, but for the next 300 meters, Kat and the old man pedaled mightily, side-by-side, and laughed with gusto rarely heard outside a little kid's birthday party.

That was the moment. Of all the temples and ruins and phad thai and elephants and monks and mountains … that is the image that will stick with me forever.

For I aspire to be that old man, pedaling down the road of life— knees knocking, bones creaking—with the exuberance and laughter of a five-year-old.

A FATHER'S TOUCH

I CALL IT "the gamble"—purposefully aiming to be in-between guaranteed lodging around sunset. For as much as I like the comfort and affordability of the guest houses in Thailand, when you pay for your lodging, your relationship is client first and guest second.

When you carry a tent on a bicycle journey, all you truly need is a four by six foot patch of flat ground.

The small secondary road wound through the forest and farm-land, a mixture of bamboo, rice fields and second-growth teak. It was a grand respite from Highway 1 not far to the east. We would be guaranteed lodging on Highway 1, but we would also be guaranteed plenty of traffic in the form of large trucks and noisy scooters.

Kat and I began looking for that flat patch soon after we had been passed by a speeding Toyota pickup—with an elephant in the back. It was our first double take in Thailand.

Our "What was that about?" reactions were soon answered by another speeding truck filled with teak logs—tree poachers. Logging of hardwoods was outlawed in Thailand in 1989, but continues throughout the country. Poachers use elephants to drag cut logs out of the forest to the road where trucks wait to speed them away.

The sun was now low in the sky and the light was approaching the level when mosquitoes rise to feast on those without shelter.

We came to the edge of a small village. Most parcels were fenced off. There was no store or restaurant to stop and inquire about lodging. Our options were running out.

Gambling sometimes pays off and sometimes doesn't. I imagined us pitching a tent in a bog near the side of the road as the shadows of night fell.

We passed a couple standing outside their home and the woman smiled at us. Nearby was a tamarind tree orchard. We stopped and asked if we could pitch our tent under the trees.

They indicated that the land wasn't theirs, but belonged to the old man next door.

He had just arrived home and parked his bicycle around the back of the simple wooden home. He was thin and slightly hunched over and blind in one eye.

The neighbors introduced us and explained our request.

He smiled and nodded his head. He showed us where we could pitch our tent and then led us through the house to the bath and toilet. It was a small structure tacked on to the end of the house. There was a simple squat toilet and a square cement water trough with a small bucket to use for bathing. A tiny mirror and a hair brush hung on the woven bamboo wall; a couple of toothbrushes wedged into the cracks.

We thanked the old man and crawled into our tent, delighted to be clean after a dusty, muggy day of cycling. We wondered if we'd seen the last of him.

But the smell of smoke and glow of a fire drew us out. He sat outside on a wooden bench next to a table and his wife sat nearby on a stool. Dressed simply in pants and an embroidered sweatshirt, she had a quiet elegance about her. Her hair was dark with wisps of gray.

The old man sat us down on the bench and then sat right next to me. He wore gray slacks and a gray shirt with a purple polyester coat. His breath was sweet and smelled of sticky rice. He talked to me, although I did not understand a word. And he felt my arms, in a gentle manner, like someone inspecting a prized horse. Then he put his strong hand on my shoulder and massaged it.

I was taken aback, for it is the exact way my father touches me when I come home to visit—first the forearms then the shoulder. When I was in high school, it made me uncomfortable, "Dad, that's just weird," I'd say. Later, I tolerated it.

But looking at this stranger's face in a small village in Thailand, I felt embraced without being hugged. I felt, for lack of better words, "in touch".

A couple of boys showed up, fascinated with our bicycles, and then more neighbors dropped by.

We sat out by the fire for hours. We sang a bit, coaxed on by a neighbor who was on her second bottle of Thai whiskey. She sang a chorus of what sounded like an old folk song. I sang a chorus from the musical "The Fantastics" and she laughed after every phrase, which made everyone else laugh, including me. Laughter is the perfect universal language. We don't speak it often enough.

A young girl dropped by whose boyfriend in Bangkok had taught her some English. Through her we learned that our hosts were childless and had lived in the village all their lives. After many attempts, we finally understood the old man's joke that if I relieved myself during the night, his tamarinds would be that much sweeter.

The fire finally died, the neighbors said their goodbyes and Kat and I retired to our tent under the tamarind trees. We fell asleep to the chirps, buzzes and whistles of unknown birds and bugs.

Our perfect night's slumber was interrupted at 2 AM when a stray dog came upon our tent and began to bark. Soon we had chorus of village dogs. I made the mistake of getting out of the tent to try and quiet them, which only spurred them on to bark with more gusto. An hour later they abruptly stopped for no apparent reason.

We rose with the sun. The village was already alive with sounds: roosters crowing, the whirs of bicycle wheels and the whine of a scooter or two, knives chopping fresh vegetables, dogs barking, children laughing.

We wondered if we'd see the old man before we left. As we rolled our loaded bikes out of the orchard, there he was with his wife standing outside the door.

The old man gave us a bag of freshly cooked sticky rice. And then he gave me a hug—the first I had received in Thailand.

I looked at the old man. I didn't even know his name.

We did not share a language. We barely had anything close to what you would call a conversation.

Yet in those brief moments around the fire, I came to understand my own father's touch and an old man got to feel what it was like to have a son.

LAOS: ON AND OFF "THE CIRCUIT"

PANIC. I SHOT straight up from my sleeping bag. My heart thumping in my chest. An insanely bright light accompanied by a horrifically loud thunderous noise forced me to cup my ears.

Confusion. I had no idea where on earth I was or what I should do. But in that instant I knew I was going to die.

The earth rumbled; dust and leaves blew up against the tent.

Then, in a series of quick flashes, my brain began to weave the foreign bits of information together.

I am in a tent. Kat is here with me. We are in Laos. We are in a small Hmong village in the North. We are camped in a market stall on the precipitous edge of the road. And *that* was a long haul trucker.

After a couple of deep breaths, we were both able to laugh about it.

What a contrast to our guesthouse lodging in Luang Prabang, a World Heritage city and the old capital of Laos. We arrived from Northern Thailand after a two-day boat ride on the Mekong, our bikes lashed to the top of the large water taxi filled with foreigners. There we had the best cup of coffee I've had outside of Seattle and the best chocolate croissant I've had anywhere on the planet.

The cobblestone streets were packed with tourists and travelers from every corner of the globe. Bars, cafés, restaurants and
bakeries—our days were filled with eating, visiting the wonderfully
restored *wats*, and strolling through the markets.

Every country has its circuit—that popular route taken by
most of the tourists and backpackers. In India it is the triangle—
Delhi to Agra to Jaipur with a sojourn out to Jaisalmer for those
who have more time. In Turkey it is Istanbul to Ephesus (Ephes) to
Cappadoccia. The smaller the country, the better the odds that every
tourist and traveler is on the same route.

Laos is a small country with few paved roads so the "circuit" is
well defined. Beginning in the north, you enter Laos from Chang
Kong, Thailand via a five-minute boat crossing of the Mekong. From
there you pick up a tourist boat at Houei Xai for a two-day float
down the Mekong to the old capital city of Luang Prabang. Next
stop is south to Van Vieng or "chill-out town" for the backpacker
crowd. Then it's on to the present capital city of Vientiane before
returning to Thailand.

Beyond the circuit you'll find it difficult to locate a cup of coffee or a guesthouse (which is why we found ourselves camped in a
market stall on the edge of the road), but you will be rewarded with
a truer look into the lives and culture of the people of Laos.

Having just spent over a month and a half in bustling Thailand,
the quiet was both welcomed and a bit unnerving. Laos is the least
densely populated country in Southeast Asia. Its lack of development makes it a bicycle traveler's dream destination.

When we cycled north out of Luang Prabang (the fourth largest
city in Laos) along the main highway, we counted twenty vehicles per
hour on the road. Two days later as we turned east, the traffic plummeted to twenty vehicles per day along a paved road barely wide
enough for your average American SUV.

Our loop in Northern Laos took us on a roller coaster ride through Hmong villages and forestland. Each day of pedaling was a series of climbs near gurgling streams and through villages where Hmong children often ran screaming from us, only to turn and wave with enormous grins on their dirt-streaked faces once they were safely near their family's bamboo dwelling.

The lack of traffic allowed us to delight in the individual sounds of the forest and village: the laughter of kids, the chirps and trills of forest birds, the rhythmic thwacking of bundled *khem* (elephant grass) as villagers removed the seeds in order to make brooms, and the grunts and squeals of small packs of pigs crossing the road or rooting though roadside ditches.

Stores and restaurants were rare, and we often found ourselves asking around in a village for someone who could cook us a meal.

Lodging was also a challenge. In one village, after asking around, we found a local who was willing to open her home to us. We woke to the knock of the local policeman, who chided them for having unregistered foreign guests and required them to purchase a permit (for which we later reimbursed them).

In another village we set up our tent outside of a Hmong family's home. Early the next morning I awoke to the sound of a man speaking at us through our mosquito netting. He was wearing what I swore was a bright pink feather boa. "It must be the crazy uncle," I thought to myself. Then I glanced past his shoulder to spy another man with a machine gun.

It was the local police, once again concerned with the foreigners in their midst. But we pedaled out of the village without incident after our host family had fed us packaged noodles they had purchased especially for their guests.

We pedaled South over a high pass and down into the plains of Phonsavan. This region is littered with unexploded ordinance, leftover from "the Secret War." From 1964-1973 U.S. planes flew over 10,000 missions, dropping over a million bombs—over one ton of explosives for every man, woman and child in Laos. The cluster bombs opened up and rained "bombies" the size of baseballs, packed with ball bearings. Some ten to thirty percent didn't detonate and pose an enormous risk to kids and farmers over thirty years later.

We took the time to explore the Plain of Jars, where groupings of enormous stone urns (some weighing several tons) loom on the bare plateau. No one knows for sure who made them or for what reasons ... Burial urns? Whiskey vats? Victory monuments?

Our paths were lined with modern stone markers delineating which areas had been cleared of mines and bombs.

The region was hard on us emotionally. Yet I can't imagine understanding the modern history of Laos and the struggle of its amazingly resilient people without spending time there.

Our loop ended back onto the main highway. In two weeks, we had not seen a single traveling cyclist and only a handful of travelers. Now, within twenty minutes, we had met six other cyclists. We were back on the circuit.

We descended from the mountains of northern Laos along the Nam Song River and arrived in Van Vieng, that place know to back-packers as "chill-out town".

When I say backpackers, I'm not referring to those who climb mountains and trod dusty trails and know their way around a Swiss Army knife. The backpackers I've observed in Laos are young tour-ists who have shunned the Samsonite with wheels for the suitcase with shoulder straps. The only time they walk with this backpack is from the bus station to the nearest taxi or *tsong-tao* that whisks them away to a guesthouse, where they deposit their backpack and then congregate in outdoor restaurants drinking beer and consulting their travel guides to see where the bus will take them next.

Van Vieng is filled with guest houses, Internet cafés, tour companies and restaurants. The locals give the backpackers what they desire, and from my observation, they desire ... television. Why converse with people from all over the globe when you can chill to *Kill Bill*?

The most obscene or hilarious example, depending how you look at it, are two restaurants, one on each side of the street, which have lounge seating so that patrons can lie down and eat while watching reruns (and I'm not making this up) of the television sitcom *Friends*—morning, noon and night.

We observed one young backpacker nursing a beer, eyes glazed over, his large posterior facing the street. He was still there when we walked by six hours later.

Fortunately the town is small and the surrounding area is dominated by dramatic karst mountains.

Kat and I decided on a river trip. We paid for the rental of inner tubes and hopped into a *tsong-tao* (two-bench truck/taxi) with five others. A quiet float down a scenic river seemed the best way to escape the tourist slums of Van Vieng.

How wrong we were. There were other tsong-taos filled with other foreigners with inner tubes and we all piled out and plopped into the cool waters of the Nam Song. Dozens of tubes drifted downriver like so many donuts in a vat of grease.

Yet the scenery was stunning enough to make me forget we were surrounded by fellow sunscreen-slathered foreigners or *falangs*.

Until we rounded the corner. I can only say that if Francis Ford Coppola were to make a movie about backpackers in Southeast Asia, this would be his *Apocalypse Lao*.

On the banks of the Nam Song were make-shift bamboo bars where over a hundred backpackers had parked their inner-tubes in bamboo stalls. Women in bikinis and shirtless men drank beer and watched their friends climb a sixty-foot tall, bamboo tower then swing out on a rope and dive, or jump, or belly flop into the water. Eight-year-old boys fished foreigners out of the river with long bamboo poles and cries of "Beer Lao, Beer Lao." Bob Marley, Queen and technopop blared out of enormous speakers.

Meanwhile in the same waters, local women in traditional dress waded into the shallow parts of the river collecting river moss to dry for food.

There was not a single peaceful stretch of the three-hour journey. Every bend in the river supplied a new place to setup a sound system and a makeshift pier stocked with cases of beer. I talked with another traveler who informed me that three years ago none of this was here: "No thatch river-side bars, no diving towers, no eight-year-olds selling beer. Just the Nam Song and some of the most stunning scenery in Laos."

How could it all be aesthetically trashed so quickly?

"That was awesome," a young woman exclaimed as she shouldered her inner tube. "We floated down yesterday as well. Best thing we've done in all of Southeast Asia." What did you think?

I didn't know what to say. I was surprised and saddened by her enthusiasm for the gross spectacle we'd all floated through. But mostly, I felt really, really old.

"Not bad", I lied as I shouldered my own inner tube. "Not bad at all."

Laos is changing fast. For good and for bad.

The Chinese are helping to build a massive highway in northern Laos. Once that road is finished, much of Laos' forests will go the way of Thailand's forests, logged and transported to lucrative markets.

Power lines are going into many villages that have never had electricity before. Guesthouses are popping up. Adventure travel companies are staking their claims to authentic experiences along virgin routes.

Five years ago the streets of the capital city Vientienne were filled with bicycles, with the occasional scooter. Now scooters outnumber bicycles a hundred to one.

Laos is changing so fast that the latest guidebook is already out of date before it hits the shelf.

Progress? Mindless development? Inevitable change?

Whatever your view or opinion ... the time to visit Laos (on or off the circuit) is now.

WHAT'S IN A NAME?

Names are important. They identify us. They set us apart. But they may also connect us as well.

On August 4, 1961 Bob and Noni Weir decided to name their second son William Robert Weir. I have grown up answering to a number of variations of that name … Billy, Bill, Billy-Bob (only my grandmother got away with calling me that), Will, etc. Willie is the one that has stuck over the long run.

When I was in sixth grade, my class of twenty-five fellow students included two other Billys, Billy Keenan and Billy Zimmerman. The three of us had a special bond because we shared the same first names. We were the Brothers Billy … Billy K., Billy W. and Billy Z.

I remember wondering (while waiting for the recess bell to ring) what it would be like to meet someone with my name … first and last. What would it be like to look into the eyes of William Weir? Would he be like me?

That memory flooded back into my thoughts as I took the ferry ride from Manitoulin Island to Bruce Peninsula in Southern Ontario while on a bicycle journey across Canada. As I pushed my loaded bike into the ferry terminal I passed a phone booth. On a whim I squeezed in and paged through the phone book. As luck or fate would have it, my index finger found a "Weir, William" listed in the nearby town of Wiarton.

I dialed the number and a woman answered. I explained the odd reason for my call and the woman said she would be delighted if another William Weir dropped by the house. As I pedaled across town, I wondered about this strange encounter. Would sitting across the table from William Weir (the Canadian version) be like looking in a mirror? Would we have some sort of cosmic connection? Would I like the other William Weir? What if he was a jerk?

I found the address, walked up to the door and knocked. Violet Weir, a frail woman in her eighties answered the door. She invited me into the kitchen and poured me a cup of tea. She asked me to tell her about my journey and what I thought of Canada and Canadians. About ten minutes later I finally asked if her husband would be joining us.

"Oh, no. William's been dead for eight years, God rest his soul."

After a third cup of tea and learning that I had absolutely nothing in common with the deceased William Weir (he never learned to ride a bicycle) I left the house feeling rather silly. What was I expecting? Names were simply random labels.

Or so I thought, until I learned of another William Weir ... one who traveled the world on a bike ... one that made his living writing about travel ... one who had begun his long distance cycling adventures with a bicycle journey across the United States.

The similarities were so striking that the way we learned of each other was through a letter someone wrote him. The writer thinking he was me.

When we first talked to each other on the phone in 1996 I was days away from leaving on a five-month journey through the Balkans. I almost dropped the phone when the other William Weir informed me that in three weeks time he was leaving on his own multi-month bicycle journey through the Balkans, What are the odds that two people would share the same name, passion, career, and then plan identical bicycle journeys at same time?

We didn't meet up on that trip, but when I returned home there were three postcards from him ... all mailed from cities that I'd passed through.

Now jump ahead almost ten years and many bicycle journeys later by the duo of Williams. I'm sitting in an Internet café in Chiang Mai, Thailand and I get an email from William Weir. He has finished up a trip in India and is flying to Bangkok and heading North towards Laos.

I realize by looking at his itinerary that we will be cycling the same stretch of highway (albeit from different directions) he from the south, me from the north, and if all went well, our paths would intersect somewhere between the towns of Mae Hong Son and Mae Sariang.

A week passed and Kat and I arrived in Mae Hong Son. An email from the other William confirmed he was heading north. Less than a hundred miles separated us.

This was more than bizarre. This was a meeting arranged by the travel gods.

As Kat and I pedaled along the hilly, winding landscape, I kept imagining spotting a cyclist, loaded down for travel, gracefully rounding a bend. There would be hugs and laughter—the perfect cap on a strange story of cosmic coincidence.

When we stopped for lunch I left our bikes out near the road and opted out of some interesting side trips in fear that in those short moments my traveling twin would pass us by.

But hundreds of curves and hills and a day's journey later, we pedaled into the town of Kuhn Yuam. No sign of him.

That night I emailed him from an Internet café ... an Internet shack, actually, filled with twelve-year-old Thai boys playing video games.

"Where are you?"

When we packed up the next morning the feeling of excitement was gone. "He's gone. I feel it in my gut and I don't know how he passed us."

We coasted down the dusty main street of Khun Yuam and on the left hand side was a hotel. A rundown place we'd quickly passed on, assuming it was closed.

I couldn't help myself. I put on my brakes and turned around. I walked up to the unattended front desk and opened up the guest register.

There, standing out in bold block letters in the register, surrounded by entries in Thai script was "William Weir".

At the exact moment that I was emailing him from an Internet shack—he was checking into the only other hotel in town, a mere two blocks away.

I laughed. The travel gods laughed.

Kat and I pedaled out of town ... and William Weir simultaneously cycled north and south along a forested highway in Northern Thailand.

ZEB

FOR OVER TEN years, Kat and I have traveled by bicycle together. I've shared our travels in *Adventure Cyclist* magazine, on public radio and with thousands of folks around the country who have come to my travel presentations. I'm not sure why I haven't admitted it before, but there has been a third party on many of our adventures.

Maybe it's because certain things should remain a secret—or that two traveling the lonesome back roads is more dramatic than three—or just maybe it's due to the fact that I'm forty-six years old and the traveling companion I'm eluding to is a stuffed animal.

Zeb joined us in a roundabout way. Kat was going to attend a friend's baby shower, and purchased a small stuffed animal to attach atop the gift she was giving. But by the time she got home from the store, she was having second thoughts.

"That is the damn cutest Zebra I have ever seen."

Next came the justification.

"He is way too cute for a little kid to truly appreciate. I mean, this poor little zebra is just going to get chewed and drooled on and then have his head bitten off by their dog. It would be a crime to send him off to what amounts to a death sentence."

The gift was delivered sans zebra. Zeb stayed with us.

He lived on top of Kat's computer monitor for almost a year. He developed quite the personality. He didn't like long workdays (zebras prefer sipping cappuccinos at outdoor cafés), he cursed at the stupidity of some of Kat's clients, *and* he demanded to know when we were going on our next trip.

How could we refuse? At six inches tall and weighing in at eight ounces, he was born to ride.

Zeb (he also answers to "Zebediah" and "Zebles") lounges most of the time, attached to the handlebars of Kat's bike with a small bungee cord so he can enjoy the view. Except when we pedal into small villages. He usually hides out inside the front handlebar bag (Zeb has always been paranoid about being kidnapped by a gang of four-year-olds).

I might not have been willing to admit to traveling with a cute little mascot if I hadn't met so many other travelers toting one along as well.

Stuffed monkeys, teddy bears, Gumbys, even a traveling Barbie. All carried by bicycle travelers ranging from eighteen to seventy-two years old.

Some travelers carry them openly—proudly displaying their fuzzy travel companions on their back racks. One gentleman even had a small helmet for his stuffed Secret Squirrel, of television fame. Others are more discreet, not admitting to having a "little friend" until late night drinks around a campfire. It makes me wonder how many other travelers I've encountered who have undeclared travel companions.

Why would a group of intrepid adult travelers be prone to carry a child's toy?

I suppose for those of us who come from auto-centric cultures … why wouldn't we? The establishment claims we are already riding a child's vehicle. There is also something about the simple, vulnerable and carefree nature of a bicycle journey that has its roots in childhood.

Trip mascots can also play an important social role.

Zeb serves as a go between. Kat and I often communicate with each other through Zeb. On a multi-month journey, sometimes a third party (stuffed or not) can be of help.

Our little stuffed mascot is often attributed with saying things that need to be said, but would otherwise remain unspoken.

For example:

"Zeb thinks we pedaled over one too many passes yesterday."

Translation: "Willie, this is a bike trip, not a death march. A little less testosterone please."

"Zeb wants to see the sunrise."

Translation: "Kat. We've been oversleeping and are missing the cool part of the day to ride."

"Zeb requests that we splurge on a nice room in Istanbul."

Translation: "Willie, you cheap bastard. If you want to stay married, get out the credit card."

"Zeb says you should put on some deodorant. Pronto!"

Translation: (none needed).

He is also a little link to home—a connection to what we've left behind and a heck of a lot cheaper than a cell phone. I don't mean to demean the little guy. He has worked his way into our hearts. I didn't realize just how much until a cold, rainy night in the Okefenokee Swamp in Georgia.

Kat and I were camped in our tent at the state park campground, surrounded by motor homes and campers.

I heard an uncharacteristically loud rummaging in our panniers.

"Where's Zeb? I can't find Zeb!" Kat frantically exclaimed.

We dug through every bag and pannier. Nothing. There are only so many places you can look in a four-by-six tent.

"I took him off the front of the bike when it started to rain this afternoon. Did I put him on the back rack and forget to pack him away?"

Kat was despondent. I fortunately refrained from saying, "It's just a stuffed toy."

I couldn't believe that Kat could be so upset. But at 2 AM, with a cold drizzle still pattering away at our tent, I was awake. It tore me up. Yes. He was just a little stuffed animal, but I was genuinely unnerved. My hearts was racing. My gut felt queasy.

I tried to put the whole thing out of my mind. But hours later I lay there thinking about the cute little guy, wet and muddy, in some ditch along the side of the road, staring up into a bleak Georgia winter's night and thinking, "They'll come get me."

In the morning, Kat and I packed up camp in silence. We both knew that trying to retrace the last forty miles of our route looking for Zeb was a futile exercise.

Kat went digging in her rear pannier for a bandana and let out a scream.

"Zeb!"

Kat thrust her hand, with Zeb tightly clutched in it, up toward the sky.

Somehow our little buddy had managed to remain undiscovered during hours of searching, only to miraculously reappear.

After hugs and celebrations, Zeb was secured with an extra mini bungee cord to Kat's handlebars. It made his stomach pooch out in a rather unflattering manner, but he didn't seem to mind.

We were back on the road. The three of us. All was right with the world.

I know that some folks will read this and think, "Wow. Those two need to have a kid or at least a few sessions of psychoanalysis."

But there are others—travelers with stuffed mascots, cyclists with small inanimate friends that connect them to home while they explore foreign places—who know exactly how we felt.

Zeb currently sits on his perch on top of Kat's computer monitor. He is our physical reminder that anyone or anything that stays put too long gathers dust.

It's time to start packing. Zeb's ready for another adventure ... and so are we.

ENRIQUE'S COLOMBIA

WE PEDALED INTO the tiny town square, our bodies soaked with sweat from an all-day climb up an unpaved road. A local pointed out the *hospedaje* (small hotel), but the soldiers behind the sandbagged check station on the corner waved us over. One of the soldiers rested his arms on the assault rifle slung across his chest while he looked at our passports.

He glanced over at our loaded touring bikes, then shook his head slowly and said, "What are you doing here? Haven't you talked to your embassy?"

We hadn't.

Why were we in this obscure mountain town high in the Andes, in what many people perceive as the most dangerous country in the world?

It began with an email, one of dozens that pop into my inbox every day. It was from a woman who had listened to my commentaries over the years on public radio station KUOW in Seattle.

She had heard that Kat and I were going to travel to Colombia. In a non-chalant manner, she wrote she had a friend who she thought we might like to meet. His name was Enrique Peñalosa. I glanced at the name again. *Oh, my God!*

For those who don't recognize the name, let me put this into perspective. Imagine someone contacting you out of the blue and saying, "I've got a friend who is a cyclist. He is kind of an interesting guy, and I thought you might like to meet him. His name is Lance ..."

To those in the bicycle advocacy world, Enrique Peñalosa enjoys Lance Armstrong status. He is the former mayor of Bogotá, the capital of Colombia, a city of over seven million people.

What happened under Enrique Peñalosa's leadership is referred to as the Bogotá Miracle. A crime-ridden, polluted, congested, barely livable city was turned around through an amazing series of programs.

Libraries were built in the poorest of neighborhoods. Bollards were erected to keep cars from parking on the sidewalks, giving the streets back to the people. Bus rapid transit was developed throughout the city. Over 350 kilometers of bike paths were constructed, and a Sunday tradition called "Ciclovía" was greatly expanded. Every Sunday (fifty-two weeks out of the year), over seventy miles of arterials in the city are closed to vehicular traffic from 7 AM until 2 PM and turned over to the people of Bogotá. Over 1.5 million people participate in this grand weekly civic event that has no rival on the planet.

We met him in his office north of downtown. Enrique Peñalosa is a tall, strikingly handsome man with salt-and-pepper hair and the engaging presence of a seasoned public official.

He didn't waste any time and quickly asked to see our route.

Every traveler we'd had contact with, every blog we had read, every article, guidebook, pamphlet and website had said the same thing,:"Colombia is much safer than it used to be, but you *must* travel on the main highways only. Don't even think about straying off these arterial roads." We had been disappointed to learn this, but had resigned to the fact that we didn't have the back road options we so enjoyed on our other travels.

Enrique pondered our route as we traced it on the map.

He frowned. "You won't see my country this way. This is the way for trucks."

His finger traced the thinnest of lines.

"This is Colombia. Most of these roads aren't paved. This one here. You'll have to walk your bike up this road."

He then proceeded to trace out routes all over Colombia, years worth of pedaling.

We asked about the guerillas.

"You may encounter FARC, but two Americans on bicycles, I don't think they'd know what to do with you."

That brief meeting transformed our journey. Anyone else could have said the same thing, but it wouldn't have carried the same weight. Our respect for this man allowed his words to propel us past our fears and turn off the main highway.

So what I should have said to the soldier when he asked what we were doing in his small mountain town was, "Enrique sent us."

Ask the general public what comes into their mind when you mention Colombia and they'll say—kidnapping, FARC, drugs, paramilitary, murder.

For decades Colombia has been the country that travelers (including cyclists) fly over or express-bus through on their epic journeys in South America.

A journey from Bogotá to Medellín on the main highway could have been pedaled in five days. Our Enrique-inspired route took over three weeks. The main highway follows the valleys or climbs the gradual ridges. The main highway might gradually climb from 3,000 to 10,000 feet, whereas the alternate route roller-coasters up and down the river drainages, forcing you to pedal upwards of 25,000 vertical feet to get to the same destination.

It became hard to remember when we last saw a flat piece of road. Hours and hours of climbing each day—ascending 5,000 feet only to descend 4,000 feet and then repeat. One evening we were so exhausted that we set the tent near a farmhouse on a rocky patch of ground at an angle so steep it was comical. We didn't care. We gnawed on some cold food in our packs and fell asleep within seconds. The next morning I urged Kat to chant, "*Yo soy una machina*" (I am a machine), as we finally peaked over our first of many passes over 10,000 feet.

But, oh, the rewards for our efforts—hillsides of a thousand shades of green, parrots and macaws, the sweet smell of coffee blossoms, picturesque towns perched on mountaintops.

We encountered a man named Moncho on our first week out. He invited us to his farm and took us on a walking tour of his land—dappled with coffee, sugarcane and cattle. We ended up back at his small humble dwelling where his wife and mother had prepared a lunch of grilled meat, rice and beans, grilled potatoes, fresh milk and blackberry juice.

We sat dazed after stuffing ourselves. Moncho motioned to the cot in the next room with a contented smile. It was time for us to take a nap.

A quick glance at our map the next morning said "easy day". Herveo was at the same elevation as the town we were leaving. A closer look revealed two river crossings, which meant two major climbs.

The steep dirt/mud road wound its way through coffee fields. Small waterfalls spilled over our path. Hummingbirds zoomed through the trees while vultures lazily soared high above our heads.

We limped into Herveo not long before sunset. They knew we were coming. Not just the military or the police, but the whole town. Our welcoming committee included the head of the cultural department, the middle school IT/English teacher, and the local historian, a short, barrel-chested man with a bright smile and weepy eyes.

They had already arranged for a room at the local hospedaje and sat us down at the town-square bakery for coffee. The golden light of late afternoon spilled across the cobblestone square. Several horses stood tethered outside the hat shop, while men swept up coffee beans that had spent the day drying in the sun. A couple of tall wax palms towered over the white-washed Catholic church. Kids laughed as they ran across the square headed for the ice cream vendor.

"Do you have many tourists visit here?" I asked.

"Yes," the cultural minister beamed. "Two." He pointed to us and laughed.

For the next two days the little town of Herveo reached out and gave us a collective hug.

We toured every square inch of the town, and were never allowed to buy our own cup of coffee. We were invited to be special guests on the local radio station (99.5 FM). The studio was a tiny room donated by the hospital. The announcers were schoolteachers who spun vinyl on a child's record player while holding a microphone over the spinning disc.

Our hosts treated us to dinner at both of Herveo's restaurants that night, as a cold mist fell over the town square. It was Saturday night, but the sidewalks were still rolled up by 10 PM.

Every adventure has its magical place—a destination that your mind repeatedly returns to long after the journey is over.

Herveo is a tiny town that may never make it into a guidebook, yet it looms large in our memories of Colombia

We left the next morning after hugs and two cups of coffee, only to discover that we had escorts. The whole town was concerned for our safety (the road we had entered town on was considered dangerous—many of the locals had not traveled on it for over a decade, so they sent a couple of policemen on a motorcycle to guard us. For the next five hours they putted along beside us, or motored on ahead to the next bend in the road and waited. We bought them lunch when we reached the closest military checkpoint. They turned back to Herveo, while we pedaled on to the city of Manizales.

The roads Enrique had recommended were always a physical challenge. It was slow going. But the lack of traffic, the fresh mountain air, the sheer beauty that surrounded us, made us want to slow down even more. We called it the "art of the linger." When the woman behind the counter at one café cracked a couple of eggs into a dish and then used the steamer from a giant old Italian espresso machine to froth them into breakfast bliss, I considered slashing the tires of our bikes and declaring the trip over.

But there were more mountain towns to explore (Aranzazu, Salamina, Pácora and Aguadas). Each had a town square worthy of an extended stay.

Our route to Medellín finally forced us out to the main highway for a day, offering us a chance to experience what our journey might have been if we hadn't met with Enrique. The Pan American Highway through this section of Colombia is two lanes of curving asphalt with no shoulders. There is nothing like spending the day with hundreds of semi-trucks—whose drivers have never met a blind corner that would prevent them from passing—to make one yearn for a rock-strewn, muddy dirt track back up into the mountains.

"Get me off this thing," Kat yelled above the din of diesel motors.

We planned our escape the next morning, searching for an alternate route to Medellín as we ate breakfast at a roadside café. Nothing more than a table with wooden benches and a simple thatch roof over several wood-fired pots.

We ate what the locals ate. Eggs and *arepas*, washed down with hot chocolate. (You've got to love a country where burley truck drivers enjoy their morning cup of hot chocolate).

A man walked up to us and said, "Thank you for taking the time to visit my country. I hope you are treated well here." He then climbed into a Land Cruiser and drove off. We realized soon after that he had paid for our breakfast.

We arrived in Medellín. Another city steeped in bad media, as the former headquarters of Colombia's cocaine cartels. But good news rarely makes it onto mainstream media. Medellín is currently a safe city to visit, with art galleries, museums, parks and an eternal spring-like climate. The metro whisks you efficiently across the city. A cable car system services the poorer neighborhoods high up the hills to the north. The ride provides stunning views of the city and surrounding mountains, and shouldn't be missed.

It was in Medellín that we met our first foreign tourist. We had been traveling in Colombia for over a month. The typical traveler flies into Bogotá then busses to Medellín, next stop Cartegena. Then it's off to another South American country. Oh, what they miss!

The easy route to Cartagena was tempting—downhill and then flat all the way to the World Heritage city. But it also happened to be the main highway. We knew Enrique would have avoided it … and so did we. We turned west out of Medellín and climbed up into the Andes once again. (Colombia sports three Andean chains—Cordillera Oriental, Cordillera Occidental and Cordillera Central). It is truly the land of the granny gear.

Once we pedaled beyond Santa Fe de Antioquia (a country getaway for the wealthy of Medellín), the road was lonely and dry. Friendly soldiers at various checkpoints helped us stay on track. On the other side of the mountain pass we felt the moisture from the Caribbean as we finally descended from the Andes and out to the coastal flats. We pedaled through mile after mile of banana plantations, often sharing the road with workers pedaling to the fields.

Colombia is a country of cyclists. Their competitive racers are considered some of the best climbers in the world. We often encountered cycling club riders of all ages out for a morning ride. There is such a positive difference in traveling in a country that has a culture of cycling. Bicycles belong and are accepted on the road. In over two months we were never hassled by a motorist.

We arrived in one small town only to discover that there was no hotel or *hospedaje*. We found a woman who allowed us to camp on her property behind her house. We pitched our tent under the clothesline and next to Victor, a 300-pound pig. Victor had brothers and sisters. All of us needed a good shower.

As basic as it sounds, the lodging was offered with a smile and grace that made us feel at home.

We arrived in Cartagena a few days later. Enrique had offered us a place to stay—a flat that he shared with a business partner that wasn't being used at the time.

The old walled city of Cartagena deserves its World Heritage site status. Founded in 1533, its cobbled streets wind narrowly passed ancient churches and residences with enormous balconies.

We had the address, but had trouble finding the flat. We wandered into the Plaza de Santo Domingo. The plaza was filled with a hundred outdoor tables with umbrellas. I pointed to a plain building on the opposite side of the square and asked a waiter if that might be the place we were staying.

He looked at our road-weary clothes and mud-splattered bicycles and said,

"Oh Sir. Someone of your class would not stay in that building."

I couldn't help myself. Not one to normally drop names, I said, "I am a friend of Enrique Peñalosa."

His eyes grew wide and he sputtered, "Oh. Of course that is where you will be staying."

We were met by the staff and entered a simply, yet stunningly furnished apartment. We had to pinch each other. The waiter was right—people of our economic class wouldn't normally stay here. Considering we had previously camped next to Victor the pig, the contrast in accommodations was deliciously comical.

Our magical journey had been influenced by a man with hope and a vision for a better Bogotá, a better Colombia and a better world.

We toasted Enrique as the sun's orange glow filled the Plaza de Santo Domingo and only wished he could be there in person to receive our humble thanks.

WHAT A PRIVILEGE

I SAT IN a government office in a small town in Mexico applying for a travel visa to Guatemala. Seated next to me was a strikingly beautiful woman named Monica who was there for the same reason. At the time I was a sometimes-employed actor traveling by bicycle with less than a thousand dollars to my name. She was a professional psychiatrist with a thriving practice traveling by bus and rental car. She was dressed in silk. I was dressed in cotton and lycra. I hadn't shaved in months. She had just had her hair styled.

I walked out in five minutes with a five-year, multiple-entry visa for Guatemala. She walked out two hours later not only without a visa for Guatemala, but with an order that she had five days to leave Mexico.

It didn't make sense, except for the fact that I was a U.S. citizen and she was from Argentina.

As an American it is so easy to take travel for granted. You save some money, spin the globe, buy an airline ticket, and off you go. It's no big deal. Maybe that's why less than twenty-five percent of Americans own passports.

Or maybe it is because we are so self-focused that the average American has no curiosity about what lies beyond himself.

When I was a senior in high school I don't remember any of my classmates talking about where they were going to travel after they graduated. Everyone was talking about what kind of car they were going to buy.

I met Victor Hugo (yes, that was his real name) in the town square of Antigua, Guatemala. We quickly took a liking to each other and agreed to meet every afternoon in the park. We spent thirty minutes speaking in English and thirty minutes speaking in Spanish.

Victor had gone to university in the United States on a scholarship, so in English we talked of world politics, literature, religion, and philosophy. I had come close to failing foreign language in high school, so in Spanish we talked about the weather and sports.

Soon after we'd met, I asked Victor how he got his name.

"My mother loved the author. Lucky for me she didn't favor Rudyard Kipling."

Victor was the principal of his local school, was happily married, and had three kids. Our conversations always seemed to come back around to travel. His smile would widen and he'd get a far away look in his eyes.

"Oh, how I wish I could see the world," he would say.

"Why don't you?" I asked.

"I can't. It's impossible."

"Nothing's impossible." I answered glibly.

For the next thirty minutes I got a lesson in Third World reality. Victor had been the principal of his school for eight years. He was at the top of his earning potential. But he earned *quetzales*, not dollars.

At the current exchange rate his life savings couldn't afford him a solo plane ticket to Los Angeles, let alone a globe-trotting journey.

I remember looking at Victor as he walked down the cobblestone street after one of our meetings and thinking, "I am having the adventure that he deserves."

When we got together for the last time before I cycled south towards El Salvador, Victor looked me in the eye and said, "Travel well my friend. For you must travel for both of us."

With every journey, the value of travel increases. I become a citizen of a larger portion of this world. I listen to the news or music or read literature with an increasing depth of understanding and appreciation. And with every journey I am reminded of how fortunate I am.

In Cuba, Kat and I befriended a woman in her early twenties. Like many Cubans, Carlita was struggling to make enough money. She and her husband were raising a couple of pigs. They called them Psychosis One and Psychosis Two. At the time we traveled in Cuba, cows could not be bought or sold without permission of the government. In a way, you leased your cattle from the government. Fidel's "rent-a-cow" program I called it. Slaughtering a cow without the proper paperwork could get you thrown in jail.

Pigs were a different story. They could be freely bought and sold, so everyone we met was raising a pig or two. Even people who lived in apartments were raising pigs if there was enough room on the porch or balcony. After they sold Psychosis Two, Carlita figured they would have enough money to buy a tape recorder. And, with that tape recorder, she could further her study of languages.

This young woman already spoke Spanish, English, and French fluently and was working on German. She was majoring in tourism at the local college and loved everything about travel. One of her classes covered sports and games for tourists. They learned how to play such tourist favorites as volleyball, tennis and horseshoes.

Her instructor decided that they should all learn to water ski, but the school had very little money in the budget. They had no boat and no lake nearby. So one morning they went to the local swimming pool. They took turns putting on the skies in the deep end while their classmates stood on the other end with a rope. On the professor's command, five or six students holding onto the rope would run like hell and the person on the other end would get a two-and-a-half second ski run before plowing into the edge of the pool. The lesson and the skis did not last long.

Here was a young woman who was devoting her life to travel and tourism, yet the chances of her being allowed to visit the countries whose languages she studied and mastered were slim to none. She and her husband would have to make and save enough money (at the time they were making the equivalent of thirteen U.S. dollars a month), obtain hard-to-get visas and then harder-to-get exit permits.

We talked for hours about our countries, our lives, and our dreams.

At one point, fighting back tears she said, "I don't envy you your house, your car, your computer, your money, none of it. I envy your freedom to travel."

Four dreamers. Four would-be adventurers. Yet only one is allowed to freely travel the world.

By a cosmic roll of the dice, I was born in a wealthy nation with a stable economy and government. I am free to pedal most of this globe with few restrictions on my wanderings.

Travel isn't a right. It is a privilege—one that a majority of the citizens of the world will never experience.

When I meet the Monicas and Victors and Carlitas of this world, I am reminded of my embarrassment of riches—and of my promise never to take this wondrous privilege for granted.

LIFT OFF

I VIVIDLY REMEMBER watching the launch of the Space Shuttle Discovery. The camera zoomed in as the rockets ignited. The billowing fireballs, its shear power and energy, were awesome. But the shuttle just sat there. Was something wrong? Then there was movement, almost undetectable movement, as the shuttle struggled. It was hard to believe that this lumbering, struggling vehicle would soon be up in space and free from the force of the earth's gravity.

I love travel—the open road, the undiscovered nooks and crannies off of the tourist track. There are moments on a bicycle journey when I believe I've discovered true bliss. Yet, in order for me to take that bike trip, I first must break free from the gravitational pull of home.

Actually, Kat and I both struggle with it.

The list of things to do before we go has increased with time— getting a house sitter (and one who likes cats), finishing up work projects, getting rid of enough stuff that the house sitter has enough room to live in our house, finishing house projects so a house sitter would actually like to live in our house, paying bills, paying other bills in advance, finding people willing to fill in with several nonprofit projects we work on, shoveling a layer of compost on the garden, filing for an extension for our taxes, going to the dentist.

It wasn't always this complicated, was it?

Twenty years ago, I lived in a dumpy basement apartment. My bedroom had no windows. My roommates and I couldn't afford to turn on the heat, so you could see your breath inside the apartment from November through February. I had no furniture to speak of, unless you count a cardboard apple box used as a bedside table.

I didn't have a cat, but my roommate did. The cat had fleas. The fleas liked me ... a lot.

When I embarked on a bicycle journey, instead of pulling free of gravity like Discovery, leaving was more akin to being a hummingbird sitting on a branch and then instantly and effortlessly zooming into the sky.

I didn't leave ... I escaped.

Over ninty percent of the weight of the Space Shuttle at liftoff is fuel that will be burned in the first eight and a half minutes of flight. Almost all of its resources are used solely to break free from the pull of the earth's gravity. Leaving the earth is hard—outer space is a breeze by comparison.

It is the same for many a journey; leaving home is the hard part—the actual trip is easy in comparison.

I've known people who have been planning trips for years (decades even), and still haven't made the move.

They keep asking the same questions and search for the perfect bike. They go on countless training rides and take a language course. They buy maps and tour guides, but never take the trip.

For some the emotional pull of home is too great. Traveling means leaving friends, family and pets. And for most of us, there truly is "no place like home."

Then there is the money issue.

The financial pull of home can be even stronger than the emotional one. Finances can be the black hole of travel dreams.

Once I had a guy in his late twenties come up to me after I'd given a presentation about my five-month journey in India. Someone in the audience had asked me how much the trip had cost, and I'd stated that, excluding airfare, one thousand dollars.

This guy said, "Look. I want to travel like you do. I'll buy you dinner if I can bend your ear."

Sure.

At a nearby restaurant he took out a pad and pen and said, "A thousand bucks? I can't believe you could travel for five months on that. Tell me how?"

"Well, first I need to ask you some questions."

I took out my own notebook.

"Are you currently employed?"

"Yeah, I work for Boeing."

"Do you have a car?"

"Yes."

"Is it paid off?"

"No."

"What is your payment?"

I tried not to gasp when I heard his reply. I wrote the figure down.

"Do you have another car? Own a house? What's the mortgage payment?"

I kept asking questions and writing down the figures from his responses.

Obviously frustrated he asked, "But what does this have to do with my taking a bike trip to India?"

"Everything. When I left for India I put all, and I mean all, my possessions in a friend's closet. I had no car, no house payment, nothing. My trip through India cost one thousand dollars. Your trip through India is going to cost" ... (I paused while tallying up the figures from my notebook) ... "$17, 850, before you even set foot on the plane. That's why you aren't going to India."

He didn't.

When I speak at high schools and universities, I want to shake the students and say:

"Travel now. Get on your dumpy, used bike and go somewhere, anywhere. Those people who tell you that it doesn't get easier? They're right."

"Go before you have debts and mortgages and kids and a career. Go. The gravitational pull of home will never be lighter."

A few of them get it. But most get a car and a wallet full of credit cards.

You would think that the best way to be a world traveler would be to have no home, no base, no ties of any kind. However, I believe home grounds us as travelers. I've met too many people who severed all ties with home, only to become aimless wanderers. Traveling without a purpose or goal can become just as mind numbing as the world's worst desk job.

A man in a small village in South Africa once told me, "Travel is worth nothing unless you return home a better person for it."

I think he is right. Each trip shapes me as a person. So much of what I believe and who I am comes from the combined experiences of my journeys.

Do I long to return to the days of basement apartment living with no heat? Not a chance. I love my city, my neighborhood, my garden and my cat. But I also love to get on my bicycle and go.

That's why we're packing and storing and running a thousand errands in preparation for another trip.

I can't change gravity. The physical, financial and emotional pull of home is there and I am a fool to try and ignore it. It's better to acknowledge it, celebrate it. I consider myself fortunate to love home as much as the open road.

It takes a lot more time and energy than it did twenty years ago, but the ride is still worth it.

I don't escape anymore. I lift off.

Acknowledgments

My HEARTFELT THANKS go out to the following people and organizations.

Dan D'Ambrosio, the former editor of *Adventure Cyclist* magazine who first approached me about writing a column and named it "Travels with Willie".

Mike Deme, my current editor at the magazine. Also special thanks to Greg Siple and Aaron Teasdale.

R+E Cycles in Seattle, the home of Rodriguez. custom-made bicycles.

Ortlieb USA, for the best panniers you can put on a bike.

The Bicycle Alliance of Washington and the Cascade Bicycle Club.

Dudley Improta, Ralph Fertig, Suzanne Hanlon, Warren Smock, Dave LeRoux, Michele DeWilliam, Jim Molnar and David Branch.

My brother Jeff, who pedaled me around on the back of his Schwinn before I could pedal my own.

My mother, who sat me down almost thirty years ago and said, "Whatever you do. Whether you become a teacher or a doctor, or whether you put a pack on your back and travel the world for the rest of your life … I want you to know I consider you a success."

And thanks beyond measure to my wife, Kat Marriner, who has been both my travel and life companion for the last fourteen years. This book should truly be titled *Travels with Willie & Kat*.

WILLIE WEIR IS a columnist for *Adventure Cyclist* magazine and a traveling commentator for public radio station KUOW in Seattle. His articles on adventure travel have earned him gold and bronze Lowell Thomas Awards from the American Society of Travel Writers. He speaks at schools, universities and events around the country, advocating the bicycle as the world's best travel vehicle, as well as a vehicle for social and environmental change.

Interested in bicycle travel?
Turn your travel dream into a reality.

The material in this book originally appeared in *Adventure Cyclist* magazine, a publication of the Adventure Cycling Association. This non-profit organization based in Missoula, Montana is dedicated to "inspire people of all ages to travel by bicycle."

If you have never been on a bicycle journey but are inspired to give it a try, or you are a seasoned bicycle traveler looking for tips, maps, advice and unique guided tours, Adventure Cycling is the place to start.

Over 44,000 members and countless others use the information and inspiration provided by the premier bicycle travel organization (and largest cycling membership group) in North America.

Visit them on the Web at *www.adventurecycling.org* or call 800-755-2453.

There is no better way to see our amazing planet than by bicycle.

Adventure Cycling Association
America's bicycle travel experts